EVERYMAN'S LIBRARY
POCKET POETS

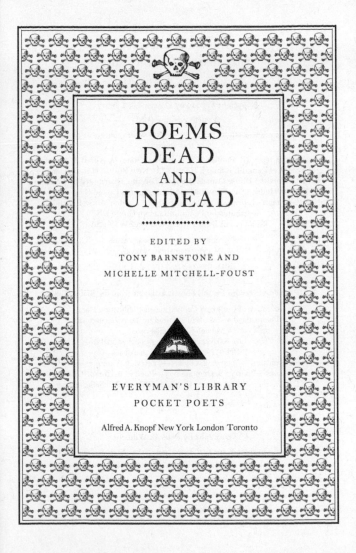

# POEMS
# DEAD
# AND
# UNDEAD

••••••••••••••••••

EDITED BY
TONY BARNSTONE AND
MICHELLE MITCHELL-FOUST

EVERYMAN'S LIBRARY
POCKET POETS

Alfred A. Knopf  New York London Toronto

THIS IS A BORZOI BOOK

PUBLISHED BY ALFRED A. KNOPF

This selection by Tony Barnstone and Michelle Mitchell-Foust first
published in Everyman's Library, 2014
Copyright © 2014 by Everyman's Library

Fourth printing (US)

A list of acknowledgments to copyright owners appears at the back
of this volume

All rights reserved. Published in the United States by Alfred A. Knopf,
a division of Penguin Random House LLC, New York, and in Canada by
Penguin Random House Canada Limited, Toronto. Distributed by Penguin
Random House LLC, New York. Published in the United Kingdom by
Everyman's Library, 50 Albemarle Street, London W1S 4BD and
distributed by Penguin Random House UK,
20 Vauxhall Bridge Road, London SW1V 2SA.

www.randomhouse.com/everymans
www.everymanslibrary.co.uk

ISBN 978-0-375-71251-7 (US)
978-1-84159-799-7 (UK)

A CIP catalogue record for this book is available from the British Library

Library of Congress Cataloging-in-Publication Data
Poems dead and undead / edited by Tony Barnstone,
Michelle Mitchell-Foust.
p.   cm.—(Everyman's library pocket poets)
ISBN 978-0-375-71251-7 (hardback)
1. Supernatural—Poetry. 2. Ghosts—Poetry. 3. Vampires—Poetry.
4. Zombies—Poetry. 5. Demonology—Poetry. 6. Horror—Poetry.
I. Barnstone, Tony, editor. II. Mitchell-Foust, Michelle, editor.
PN6110.S9P66 2014                                    2014019234
808.81'9375—dc23

Typography by Peter B. Willberg

Typeset in the UK by AccComputing, North Barrow, Somerset

Printed and bound in Germany by GGP Media GmbH, Pössneck

# CONTENTS

5

## DEVILS, GODS, ANGELS, DEATH

# INTRODUCTION
## ONE FOOT OUT OF THE GRAVE

One moment you are alive. A car accident, a piece of pork stuck in your throat, or the slow burning away of disease, and then the change comes. The blood recedes. The heart silences. The breath dies out. Something shakes out of the body with the death rattle of that last breath. This transformation is the great mystery and the source of all religion. What is it that leaves? The spirit? The words for the soul – Latin *spiritus* and Greek *pneuma* – mean "breath," and it seemed to the ancients that breath carried that mysterious pneumatic spirit that animates the body. But the moment of death isn't the story's end. Horribly, the dead body swells and farts and shifts, and the hair and nails grow after death. From such phenomena, the ancients must have asked, can the same breath that carries the spirit away carry something back into the corpse? Whether this something is infection or demon, this possession and dispossession is the great fear at the core of many monster tales. Can the dead become undead?

Can they indeed *come back* like Orpheus and Odysseus and Lazarus? Sometimes the dead are said to come back in nightmares, remnants of nature that have been suppressed, and sometimes for revenge; other times when the dead return from their descent into the earth they are (like Persephone and Inanna and Jesus) figures of the famous resurrection stories in which the planted body is actually a seed that will sprout new life.

## Zombies

At times, we call the resurrected *zombies*. They are the children of sin, the dead bursting from their caskets in the end times; or they are children of the laboratory, mothered by infections or suffering contamination in an age of HIV/AIDS and biological and chemical warfare. They come to us, things in the dark animated with unlife, and seem not to have souls, just an endless hunger to fill the emptiness inside with our tender flesh.

Fear often drives the creation of zombie tales, and of all monster tales, for that matter. What are monsters but the *unknown made flesh*? They are the *bad* unknown, *bad* because the word "monster" comes from the Latin word for "warn" (*monere*). We see in the poems of this collection the evolution of unknowns, dark figures in the family of archetypes that merit warnings. Therein lies their moniker *Monster*. And yet, the literary creation of these monsters can be a coming to terms with or a safe rehearsal of fear, as horror author Stephen King has said. Monster creators facilitate the escape from the world's crises and from "the cult of consciousness" into mythologies and "speculations of a fantasy world," according to psychologist James Hillman.

In recent depictions, zombies move faster and faster, maybe because we humans have become more and more driven in pursuit of the possible. Humans hunger more than ever – for information, for physical satisfaction, for fame. Zombies *are* hunger at a cellular level. Suppressed hunger. Cannibalistic hunger.

Yet zombies are horrible enough moving slowly, with their failing body parts falling off around them. They move beyond death perhaps because (as in Bryan Dietrich's "Zombies") "Hell / is full," or as in Kim Addonizio's poem "Night of the Living, Night of the Dead" because life itself is Hell they become zombies rising from their graves and stumbling up the hill toward the house. Thus, Addonizio winks at the reader and lets us know that these zombies are not so different from us: they are "like drunks headed home from the bar" and maybe all they want is to lie down in their drunkenness in some room while the world whirls around them, not to eat our brains after all. Maybe, in fact, the poem is really about human beings in such despair that they drink themselves into a state where they are mumbling, stumbling monsters, not unlike zombies?

In popular culture, the zombies represent different things in different generations: conformity and mind control in the Cold War era; or a disease metaphor in the era of AIDS. For Addonizio, they represent a relentless despair and self-hatred manifested in repeated self-destructive action.

*Vampires*

In England, it was common well into the nineteenth century to tie the feet of the dead to keep them from walking. Like zombies, *vampires* are the walking dead, post-humans powered by post-human desire that makes the recognizable human form *sinister*, as in Conrad Aiken's seductress vampire, with her "basilisk eyes" and "mouth so sweet, so poisonous," or that of Baudelaire, whose beauty is so great that angels would be damned for her, but who transforms after "she had sucked the marrow from [his] bones" into "a kind of slimy wineskin brimming with pus!"

We can look at ourselves as monsters and see how deeply we desire those things that quench our human, physical needs. We want to live longer; we want to eat more, kiss more, and how manipulative we can be in pursuing what we desire! Vampires are the embodiment of excess, and they, too, arise from and fall prey to infection, contamination, excess, as we see in Michael Hulse's playfully ironic song/poem "The Death of Dracula": "The fiend who bled a thousand maids / has joined the dark Satanic shades."

*Ghosts*

But what if we die and our bodies decay, unreanimated, and yet we do still not go away? Then we are yet another

14

monster, a *ghost*. Perhaps we are the residue of human ineffable sadness, wafting in the room like the scent of flowers long turned to dust.

Ghosts are our largest pool of poems to consider, probably because ghosts are the monsters of reflection. They do not frighten us because they are exaggerations of ourselves the way that zombies and vampires are. They frighten us in apparition because they ask us to remember our own coming deaths and commit us *to live*, "Because, once looked at lit / By the cold reflections of the dead / ... Our lives have never seemed more full, more real, / Nor the full moon more quick to chill" (James Merrill, "Voices from the Other World"). And they remind us that they are *out there* always reminding us.

Ghost settings, such as the Romantic graveyard of Wordsworth's poem, "We Are Seven," are as important in Gothic literature as the ghosts themselves. Traditionally, particularly in America, houses and castles are haunted, as in Robert Frost's chilling poem "Ghost House," but when the *brain* is haunted, the result is more unsettling. We can find this kind of haunting in Emily Dickinson's "One need not be a Chamber – to be Haunted," wherein the haunted body "borrows a Revolver" and "bolts the Door." And although neuropsychologist Oliver Sacks has recently described "the feeling of someone standing behind you" as a neuro-logical phenomenon, Thomas Hardy's poem "The Shadow on the Stone" puts a ghost to that feeling.

## Gods and Devils, Angels and Demons

The uncanny reanimated corpse or lingering ghost soul are a few, horrible answers to the question of what happens after that last breath rattles out in the throat, but there is horror and awe also in the idea that when one enters the land of death, the place is already popu-lated – by gods and devils, angels and demons. What is a vampire, after all, but a dark Jesus, an immortal returnee from death using his or her powers to bring us to dam-nation instead of salvation? What is Jesus, after all, but a good zombie? The horror of the zombie clawing its way out of the grave is transformed into awe when it is Jesus emerging again from the cave where his corpse had been laid out – not awful but awesome.

Many of the poems in this book pose answers to the question ... *where is the land of the dead?* Is it an actual place that you can go to, like Odysseus in Erebus – that region of darkness where the recently dead must pass on entering the underworld – and pour out offerings of blood to consult with the departed? Is it a Heaven you can go to, as in Grace Schulman's "Instructions for a Journey," seeing strange sights – a "god of fire trailing stars" and "men seventy miles high ... / with many heads / and tongues"? Or a Hell like that flaming pit from which Satan, in John Milton's *Paradise Lost*, journeys across "the womb / Of unoriginal Night and Chaos wild" to the Paradise of Adam and Eve, and in so doing forges a road between the two "paved ... By Sin and Death"?

Or is it that Heaven and Hell are realms that are mostly interior or psychological, especially after the soul has quite literally been bargained for, the paperwork has been signed and the oath sworn, as in Goethe's *Faust*, where the contract is signed in blood, since as Mephistopheles says, "Blood is a very special juice." Blood is special indeed, but little blood is spilled or exchanged when we say we are wrestling with angels and demons. We are more often than not wrestling with ourselves. Gods, devils, angels, and demons spread their influence within the realm of human consciousness. They feed on thought. Their greatest parlor tricks involve reading the human mind. They are the producers of nightmares; they inhabit nightmares; and they may *be* nightmares that import another reality into the human spirit. After all, *incubus* is another word for nightmare. Perhaps the gods are indeed the "disease" that Jung proclaimed them. They might enter us as demon lovers planting their demon seed, or like other diseases they might travel through the human mouth, causing lingual afflictions that morph our voices.

Such spirits must be exorcised, but if they are cast

17

out, to what strange realm will they go? Might we end up going there, too? Where is the land of the dead, and what lives there? The desire to answer that question has led to many poems that personify our fears into the greatest and the final monster.

## The Final Monster

We have but a few breaths left. It's time to consider the place where we began and the thing that will end us: the world's greatest unknown and the source of all the other monsters in this book: *Death*. When personified, death becomes the embodiment of foe or lover that the body wrestles in its last thrashing before the uncanny stillness of the great change. In the world's earliest poem on death, he appears in a dream to Gilgamesh's friend Enkidu, as "a towering, darkened body, / formed from a lion's head and paws, / and an eagle's talons," whereas in Emily Dickinson's "Because I could not stop for Death" he is a kind gentleman caller who picks her up to travel in a carriage toward eternity.

But what happens if the carriage gets waylaid? Then we can't accompany kind Mr. Death to eternal sleep, and we find ourselves in the Twilight Zone of half life between states of being, living in the margins, scrabbling about in graveyards and dark alleyways, attics and basements, and nursing a terrible hunger. This is why in Edgar Allan Poe's poem "The Sleeper," the speaker is absolutely desperate for Death's presence in his love Irene's tomb. He longs for her "deep sleep" when he looks at the strange vampiric coloring in her face, and desires silence from inside the tomb when he knows he can hear the dead moving around in there.

Thus it is perhaps best to put this introduction to its final rest by giving the last words on the monster Death to Robert Louis Stevenson, in whose poem death is a relief to the fatigued soul: "Soon are eyes tired with sunshine; soon the ears / Weary of utterance, seeing all is said; / ... And our sad spirits turn toward the dead; / And the tired child, the body, longs for bed" ("Death, to the Dead for Evermore").

Stevenson is best known for his novels for children and his *A Child's Garden of Verses*, which has been read by children at bedtime for over a century, after which many of them recited this prayer from the *New England Primer*: "If I shall die before I wake, / I pray the Lord my soul to take." The scary thought claws its way into the mind: what else might be waiting to take your soul? And what is it that might rise again from that final bed in the earth, shaking soil out of its eyes as it stumbles out of the cemetery and begins climbing the hill up to the house?

Enjoy this garden of monstrous verses.

TONY BARNSTONE AND MICHELLE MITCHELL-FOUST

# THE CORPOREAL
# UNDEAD

# DEPRAVED COGITATION

In the movie, two teenage boys find a naked zombie
    woman
tied to a table, and one decides to keep her as a kind of
    girlfriend.
Don't laugh. Stranger things have happened.
Someone shot Archduke Ferdinand,
a second rate monarch of a third rate nation,
and that started a world war, for Christ's sake.
In my first grade class, a boy shit his pants
and even though we could all smell it
the teacher never even noticed.
Life is full of odd events that lead to
odder circumstances. You're not supposed to ask
who tied the zombie woman to the table
in the middle of an abandoned insane asylum,
or what exactly an Archduke does,
or what kind of numskulls
are in charge of your children eight hours a day.
Just go with it, or learn the art of augury,
invest in the right tenements,
have a smoke in a haystack,
or better yet, think of the fish served in China,
cooked yet still alive, its heart beating,
its eyes sad and pleading for mercy, its tail flicking
back and forth as you reach out with your chopsticks,

then question your motives. Are you really
as good a person as you thought you were?
You are stubborn, you are greedy,
you are horny, and full of disgust and resentment for
    nearly everyone.
You wind a toy up until the spring breaks,
you kill ladybugs that fly into your house,
you wear colors and patterns that make people dizzy.
The boys in the movie get their comeuppance
in a dazzling display of gore and carnage.
Gavrilo Princip died in prison, a painful death by
    tuberculosis.
The boy in my first grade class grew up
to be a certified public accountant.
And you, before you became an orphan at forty-two –
let's suppose you got off easy, too. Easy as pie.
True enough. But everyone has a zombie tied up
in the basement. And one day it will bite
someone you love, and then she will be a zombie,
slowly rotting as you bring her gifts,
brush her hair, rub cream on her dry, brittle skin,
and make sweet, sweet love to her.

# NIGHT OF THE LIVING, NIGHT OF
# THE DEAD

When the dead rise in movies they're hideous
and slow. They stagger uphill toward the farmhouse
like drunks headed home from the bar.
Maybe they only want to lie down inside
while some room spins around them, maybe that's why
they bang on the windows while the living
hammer up boards and count out shotgun shells.
The living have plans: to get to the pickup parked
in the yard, to drive like hell to the next town.
The dead with their leaky brains,
their dangling limbs and ruptured hearts,
are sick of all that. They'd rather stumble
blind through the field until they collide
with a tree, or fall through a doorway
like they're the door itself, sprung from its hinges
and slammed flat on the linoleum. That's the life
for a dead person: *wham, wham, wham*
until you forget your name, your own stinking
face, the reason you jolted awake
in the first place. Why are you here,
whatever were you hoping as you lay
in your casket like a dumb clarinet?
You know better now. The sound track's depressing
and the living hate your guts. Come closer

and they'll show you how much. *Wham, wham, wham,*
you're killed again. Thank God this time
they're burning your body, thank God
it can't drag you around anymore
except in nightmares, late-night reruns
where you lift up the lid, and crawl out
once more, and start up the hill toward the house.

# DER TOTENTANZ (THE DANCE OF
# THE DEAD)

The warder looks down at the mid hour of night,
On the tombs that lie scatter'd below:
The moon fills the place with her silvery light,
And the churchyard like day seems to glow.
When see! first one grave, then another opes wide,
And women and men stepping forth are descried,
In cerements snow-white and trailing.

In haste for the sport soon their ankles they twitch,
And whirl round in dances so gay;
The young and the old, and the poor, and the rich,
But the cerements stand in their way;
And as modesty cannot avail them aught here,
They shake themselves all, and the shrouds soon appear
Scatter'd over the tombs in confusion.

Now waggles the leg, and now wriggles the thigh,
As the troop with strange gestures advance,
And a rattle and clatter anon rises high,
As of one beating time to the dance.
The sight to the warder seems wondrously queer,
When the villainous Tempter speaks thus in his ear:
"Seize one of the shrouds that lie yonder!"

Quick as thought it was done! and for safety he fled
Behind the church-door with all speed;
The moon still continues her clear light to shed
On the dance that they fearfully lead.
But the dancers at length disappear one by one,
And their shrouds, ere they vanish, they carefully don,
And under the turf all is quiet.

But one of them stumbles and shuffles there still,
And gropes at the graves in despair;
Yet 'tis by no comrade he's treated so ill
The shroud he soon scents in the air.
So he rattles the door – for the warder 'tis well
That 'tis bless'd, and so able the foe to repel,
All cover'd with crosses in metal.

The shroud he must have, and no rest will allow,
There remains for reflection no time;
On the ornaments Gothic the wight seizes now,
And from point on to point hastes to climb.
Alas for the warder! his doom is decreed!
Like a long-legged spider, with ne'er-changing speed,
Advances the dreaded pursuer.

The warder he quakes, and the warder turns pale,
The shroud to restore fain had sought;
When the end, – now can nothing to save him avail –
In a tooth formed of iron is caught.
With vanishing lustre the moon's race is run,
When the bell thunders loudly a powerful One,
And the skeleton fails, crush'd to atoms.

JOHANN WOLFGANG VON GOETHE (1749–1832)    29
TRANS. EDGAR ALFRED BOWRING

## ZOMBIES

It's night. Hell
is full. The dead walk the earth, and you, alone
among them, still remember the heart, the comfort
of its necessary beating. Here, trapped between
mausoleum and mortuary gate, weaponless
save for perhaps your fear, you realize you
should welcome even this, the uncertain
arc of it. All stomp and rut. All ruinous gallop.

Like ill-loved love
dolls they come – disfigured, uninhabited, rotting
to the bone above each uncapped knee, each weeping
wound gone dry. Splintered sternums no longer
suck, fractures go unknitted. Corporate, feral,
they shamble out of the dark on feet meant only
for ossuary floor, paramedic gurney, satin
foot rest. There is the smell of licorice.

Sweet forget-me-not
of formaldehyde. Necks loll back and back
till scalp meets scapula, then suddenly
a head whips forward flashing rictal gleam,
lidless teeth, open, intent on one last tongue
touch. Stumbling forward, they close on you
as you plant yourself, pristine as a leper's
femur, in the thick of all this creeping flesh.

Beside a tombstone
you make your final stand. Stealing the arm, shoulder
and all, from one who may have been your father,
    you fend
them off for a while, waving his limb before you
the way you would a dowsing rod, a hand of glory.
Living, you tire. Fighting, you fall. Past lovers
get to you first, their mouths glorious, their gums hot.
What teeth they have rip rivulets down your shins.

                    Two naked cousins –
their skin opal, bloodless, hair pale as what is now
still left of you – tear thick, stripped steaks from your
    thigh.
Shock arrives. Pain subsides. Flippering up close, close
enough to see his eyes – each slack cataract
gone black with hunger – your lost uncle, broken
backed, slams your skull against a slab until it cracks
and everything, all the forms, drowse into dark.

                    Here, where it began,
the dead continue moth-like to collect,
teeth grinding mindlessly into gristle,
ghouls unspooling your two intestines
one slow mile at a time. You can only watch
as your loss expands, a viscous pool lapping
up the world beneath you, gnawing. Consumed
at last by all that you have loved.

BRYAN DIETRICH (1965–)                    31

# DEAD MAN'S HATE

They hanged John Farrel in the dawn amid the
    market-place;
At dusk came Adam Brand to him and spat upon his face.
"Ho, neighbors all," spake Adam Brand, "see ye John
    Farrel's fate!
'Tis proven here a hempen noose is stronger than
    man's hate!

"For heard ye not John Farrel's vow to be avenged
    upon me
Come life or death? See how he hangs high on the
    gallows tree!"
Yet never a word the people spoke, in fear and wild
    surprise –
For the grisly corpse raised up its head and stared
    with sightless eyes,

And with strange motions, slow and stiff, pointed at
    Adam Brand
And clambered down the gibbet tree, the noose within
    its hand.
With gaping mouth stood Adam Brand like a statue
    carved of stone,
Till the dead man laid a clammy hand hard on his
    shoulder-bone.

Then Adam shrieked like a soul in hell; the red blood
    left his face
And he reeled away in a drunken run through the
    screaming market-place;
And close behind, the dead man came with a face like
    a mummy's mask,
And the dead joints cracked and the stiff legs creaked
    with their unwonted task.

Men fled before the flying twain or shrank with bated
    breath,
And they saw on the face of Adam Brand the seal set
    there by death.
He reeled on buckling legs that failed, yet on and on
    he fled;
So through the shuddering market-place, the dying
    fled the dead.

At the riverside fell Adam Brand with a scream that
    rent the skies;
Across him fell John Farrel's corpse, nor ever the
    twain did rise.
There was no wound on Adam Brand but his brow
    was cold and damp,
For the fear of death had blown out his life as a witch
    blows out a lamp.

His lips were writhed in a horrid grin like a fiend's on
     Satan's coals,
And the men that looked on his face that day, his stare
     still haunts their souls.
Such was the doom of Adam Brand, a strange,
     unearthly fate;
For stronger than death or hempen noose are the fires
     of a dead man's hate.

## PUCK'S NIGHTTIME SPEECH
(*From A Midsummer Night's Dream*)

Now the hungry lion roars,
And the wolf behowls the moon;
Whilst the heavy ploughman snores,
All with weary task fordone.
Now the wasted brands do glow,
Whilst the screech-owl, screeching loud,
Puts the wretch that lies in woe
In remembrance of a shroud.
Now it is the time of night
That the graves, all gaping wide,
Every one lets forth his sprite,
In the church-way paths to glide:
And we fairies, that do run
By the triple Hecate's team
From the presence of the sun,
Following darkness like a dream,
Now are frolic.

WILLIAM SHAKESPEARE (1564–1616)                    35

# ON TWO OF SIGNORELLI'S FRESCOES

1. The Rising of the Dead

I saw a vast bare plain, and, overhead,
  A half-chilled sun that shed a sickly light;
  While far and wide, till out of reach of sight,
The earth's thin crust was heaving with the dead,

Who, as they struggled from their dusty bed,
  At first mere bones, by countless years made white,
  Took gradual flesh, and stood all huddled tight
In mute, dull groups, as yet too numb to dread.

And all the while the summoning trump on high
  With rolling thunder never ceased to shake
The livid vault of that unclouded sky,

Calling fresh hosts of skeletons to take
  Each his identity; until well-nigh
The whole dry worn-out earth appeared to wake.

## 2. The Binding of the Lost

In monstrous caverns, lit but by the glare
   From pools of molten stone, the lost are pent
   In silent herds, – dim, shadowy, vaguely blent,
Yet each alone with his own black despair;

While, through the thickness of the lurid air,
   The flying fiends, from some far unseen vent,
   Bring on their bat-wing'd backs, in swift descent,
The souls who swell the waiting myriads there.

And then begins the binding of the lost
   With snaky thongs, before they be transferred
To realms of utter flame or utter frost;

And, like a sudden ocean boom, is heard,
   Uprising from the dim and countless host,
Pain's first vague roar, Hell's first wild useless word.

EUGENE LEE HAMILTON (1845–1907)

# THE BOOK OF THE DEAD MAN (MEDUSA)

*Live as if you were already dead.*
— ZEN ADMONITION

### 1. About the Dead Man and Medusa

When the dead man splays his arms and legs, he is a
     kind of Medusa.
Thinking himself Medusa, the dead man further
     splays his arms and legs.
Now he can shake it, toss it, now he can weave a
     seductive glamour into the source of all feelings,
     a glamour known to roots and to certain eyeless
     vermin of interiors.
The dead man knows the power of hair by its absence,
     hairy as he was at the near edge of immortality
     while his fame kept growing.
The dead man uses the ingredients of cosmetic
     products made just for men.
He pares his nails in the background, just as Joyce, the
     elder statesman of rainy statelessness, pictured
     the alienated artist after work.
He snips the little hairs from his nose and from inside
     the shells of his ears, for the artist must be laid
     bare in a light easily diverted.

He wears the guarded fashions of loose clothing so
that changes that might offend – the loss of a
limb or a sudden hollow in the chest – may
go undetected.
Mortal among immortals, the dead man can change
you to stone.

## 2. More About the Dead Man and Medusa

The dead man mistakes his rounded shoulders for
wings.
His shoulder blades suggesting wings, the dead man
steals a peripheral glance and shrugs, causing a
breeze.
While the dead man's nails keep growing, the dead
man has claws.
Once the dead man has lain in the earth long enough,
he will have snakes for hair.
Who could have guessed that the dead man was this
much of a woman?
Who knows better the extraneous ripple of a long
yawn?
In the theory of the dead man, nothing accounts for
his maternity.

The dead man will not move out of harm's way, nor leave his children; he repeatedly gives his life for them.

Who else may someday be beheaded by a sword made out of water and weed?

Mortal among immortals, the dead man strangles the moon in saliva.

Domed and tentacled, capped and limbed, the dead man resembles a jellyfish.

Under his wig, the dead man's waxed skull belies the soft spot on a baby's head that turns whosoever knows of it to mush.

The dead man speaks also for those who were turned into stone.

# THE SLEEPER

At midnight, in the month of June,
I stand beneath the mystic moon.
An opiate vapour, dewy, dim,
Exhales from out her golden rim,
And, softly dripping, drop by drop,
Upon the quiet mountain top,
Steals drowsily and musically
Into the universal valley.
The rosemary nods upon the grave;
The lily lolls upon the wave;
Wrapping the fog about its breast,
The ruin moulders into rest;
Looking like Lethe, see! the lake
A conscious slumber seems to take,
And would not, for the world, awake.
All Beauty sleeps! – and lo! where lies
Irene, with her Destinies!

Oh, lady bright! can it be right –
This window open to the night?
The wanton airs, from the tree-top,
Laughingly through the lattice drop –
The bodiless airs, a wizard rout,
Flit through thy chamber in and out,
And wave the curtain canopy

So fitfully – so fearfully –
Above the closed and fringéd lid
'Neath which thy slumb'ring soul lies hid,
That, o'er the floor and down the wall,
Like ghosts the shadows rise and fall!
Oh, lady dear, hast thou no fear?
Why and what art thou dreaming here?
Sure thou art come o'er far-off seas,
A wonder to these garden trees!
Strange is thy pallor! strange thy dress!
Strange, above all, thy length of tress,
And this all solemn silentness!

The lady sleeps! Oh, may her sleep,
Which is enduring, so be deep!
Heaven have her in its sacred keep!
This chamber changed for one more holy,
This bed for one more melancholy,
I pray to God that she may lie
Forever with unopened eye,
While the pale sheeted ghosts go by!

My love, she sleeps! Oh, may her sleep,
As it is lasting, so be deep!
Soft may the worms about her creep!
Far in the forest, dim and old,
For her may some tall vault unfold –

Some vault that oft hath flung its black
And wingéd panels fluttering back,
Triumphant, o'er the crested palls,
Of her grand family funerals –
Some sepulchre, remote, alone,
Against whose portal she hath thrown,
In childhood, many an idle stone –
Some tomb from out whose sounding door
She ne'er shall force an echo more,
Thrilling to think, poor child of sin!
It was the dead who groaned within.

# METAMORPHOSES OF THE VAMPIRE

The woman, meanwhile, writhing like a snake
across hot coals and hiking up her breasts
over her corset-stays, began to speak
as if her mouth had steeped each word in musk:
"My lips are smooth, and with them I know how
to smother conscience somewhere in these sheets.
I make the old men laugh like little boys,
and on my triumphant bosom all tears dry.
Look at me naked, and I will replace
sun and moon and every star in the sky.
So apt am I, dear scholar, in my lore
that once I fold a man in these fatal arms
or forfeit to his teeth my breasts which are
timid and teasing, tender and tyrannous,
upon these cushions swooning with delight
the impotent angels would be damned for me!"

When she had sucked the marrow from my bones,
and I leaned toward her listlessly
to return her loving kisses, all I saw
was a kind of slimy wineskin brimming with pus!
I closed my eyes in a spasm of cold fear,
and when I opened them to the light of day,
beside me, instead of that potent mannequin
who seemed to have drunk so deeply of my blood,

there trembled the wreckage of a skeleton
which grated with the cry of a weathervane
or a rusty signboard hanging from a pole,
battered by the wind on winter nights.

CHARLES BAUDELAIRE (1821—67)                    45
TRANS. RICHARD HOWARD

# THE REVENANT

My husband in the beams above the bed
had hid to spy on me and my young lover,
but when he saw me mounted on the cover
from behind, fell and shattered his skull – dead.
At night he'd claw out of the earth and walk,
pursued by packs of howling dogs, and kill.
We all made fast our doors in fear, but still
we heard the awful barkings as he'd stalk
outside. At last my young man took a spade
and, digging, bared the corpse suffused with blood
and swollen to enormous corpulence.
Like a great leech it wept a carmine flood,
and though its heart had suffered violence
enough, he cut it out with the blunt blade.

*From* THE GIAOUR

*After Hassan drowns the Giaour's lover, the slave-girl*
*Laila, the Giaour kills him in revenge – and is cursed.*

Who falls in battle 'gainst a Giaour
Is worthiest an immortal bower.
But thou, false Infidel! shall writhe
Beneath avenging Monkir's scythe;
And from its torments 'scape alone
To wander round lost Eblis' throne;
And fire unquench'd, unquenchable,
Around, within, thy heart shall dwell;
Nor ear can hear nor tongue can tell
The tortures of that inward hell!
But first, on earth as Vampire sent,
Thy corse shall from its tomb be rent:
Then ghastly haunt thy native place,
And suck the blood of all thy race;
There from thy daughter, sister, wife,
At midnight drain the stream of life;
Yet loathe the banquet which perforce
Must feed thy livid living corse:
Thy victims ere they yet expire
Shall know the demon for their sire,
As cursing thee, thou cursing them,
Thy flowers are withered on the stem,

But one that for thy crime must fall,
The youngest, most beloved of all,
Shall bless thee with a father's name –
That word shall wrap thy heart in flame!
Yet must thou end thy task, and mark
Her cheek's last tinge, her eye's last spark,
And the last glassy glance must view
Which freezes o'er its lifeless blue;
Then with unhallow'd hand shalt tear
The tresses of her yellow hair,
Of which in life a lock when shorn
Affection's fondest pledge was worn,
But now is borne away by thee,
Memorial of thine agony!
Wet with thine own best blood shall drip
Thy gnashing tooth and haggard lip;
Then stalking to thy sullen grave,
Go – and with Gouls and Afrits rave;
Till these in horror shrink away
From Spectre more accursed than they!

## ALL HALLOWS EVE

Standing above her open coffin,
within that pestilent place,
he stared at her colorless corpse
and stared at her lovely face.

Sensing a sense of accusation,
"Leave us alone," he said,
and the others left the mausoleum
and left him with the dead.

He placed his hand at the top of her gown
and broke the clasps apart,
staring down at the purple scar
above her silent heart.

Then he bolted the lid, locked the door,
and saw in the lightning's light
three ghouls who craved her rotting flesh
in the blackness of the night.

Maggots who dig up and eat the dead
in the pits of no-man's-land,
who scented the scent of the newly-dead,
who lunged and scratched his hand.

But he smashed them back with his walking stick,
and they staggered from the shock,
then slithered away from the dead one's tomb,
as he double-checked the lock.

But waiting near the graveyard gate,
under the hemlock tree,
a seductive vampyr smiled and said,
"Come away with me."

He saw the fangs and the famished eyes
of the tempting whore of pain,
who swiftly moved into his path
and touched his jugular vein.

But he lifted a hand of garlic flowers,
and the creature jerked and hissed
into the winds of the coming storm
and vanished in the mist.

At the edge of town, he saw the monster
nearing the torch-lit gate,
looking for its human god,
looking for its mate.

Enraged by the thunder's thunder,
it stepped away from its place,
but calmly he grabbed the flaming torch
and burned its ugly face.

Later he heard the werewolves howl,
up along the ridge,
as suddenly they blocked his path
before the wooden bridge.

Ravenous, they moved to strike,
but it was far too late;
he lifted up a silver bullet,
then his .38.

He fired at the alpha-wolf,
hitting the vicious gray
and blowing apart its little brain
as the others ran away.

Nearing his gate, he saw the daemon,
but never broke his stride,
and when it saw his hollow eyes,
it nodded, and stepped aside.

At last, the storm fell from the night,
as he entered the house of pain,
it fell in torrents, flashed and crashed,
and pounded sheets of rain.

Upstairs he found the silent ghost
sitting alone, undressed,
with the sharp and bloodless knife
protruding from her chest.

Being the one he'd just entombed,
his daughter, the jilted bride,
who'd come back home to nothing
but a shocking suicide.

The specter pointed at her heart,
but he stared across the room,
into the mirror, into his eyes,
each an empty tomb.

No wonder the creatures had cowered away,
and surely they were right,
those predators of human flesh,
those vermin of the night.

For they could only murder the body,
the part but not the whole,
but he was a far more deadly thing:
the assassin of his soul.

The storm fell down from the blackest night,
over the house of pain,
the torrents flashed and thunder-crashed
and pounded the slashing rain.

# THE DEATH OF DRACULA
a song from *Aids: The Musical*

> The poor Transylvanian is dead,
> that lay with the little baggage.
>
> PERICLES IV. 2

The Transylvanian is dead,
    That's too bad.
A crucifix above the bed
and garlic wreathed about his head –
    what a lad.

The Transylvanian's deceased.
    Such a shame.
Invite the neighbours to the feast.
We'll have a party for the beast.
    What a game.

His last words (says the nurse) were: *Damn*
    *Bram Stoker.*
The doctor claims he said: *Fuck Bram.*
*Bram sucks. I suck. Therefore I am.*
    Some joker.

You're sure there isn't some mistake?
        This *is* death?
I wish we'd brought a bloody stake.
Just keep your speeches for the wake.
        Save your breath.

It's true he's looking rather grey.
        Almost blue.
He doesn't look himself today.
Off-colour. Yes, he's dead, I'd say.
        Wouldn't you?

So even Dracula got Aids.
        I never.
The fiend who bled a thousand maids
has joined the dark Satanic shades.
        For ever.

Even Count Dracula could die.
        Fancy that.
He doesn't look too spruce or spry.
Oh Lord, I think I'm going to cry.
        For a bat.

I never knew the Count *could* kick
        the bucket.
They tell me he was really sick.
They do say: once you've sunk your prick,
        you're suckered.

Poetic justice, eh? King Lear
and that. You long for what you fear.
Let's go. He'd laugh to see us here,
    all weeping.
We'll leave him dead upon his bier.
    (Or sleeping.)

SARAH WINCHESTER, 23 YEARS DEAD,
WATCHES *HOUSE OF DRACULA*
(*in which Dracula, The Wolfman, and Frankenstein's
Monster arrive at Dr. Edelman's house for treatment*)

Is it safer when all the monsters gather
inside one house: one place to summon

and fear? The sweep of the Count's black
wing – a premonition at the doctor's door,

who answers, of course, who lets him in,
takes him down the basement stairs. Wide

as cemetery gates – the entrance to oblivion.
We don't ask why: the doctor with his shock-

white beard, his coffin full of Transylvanian
soil. Our bodies, too, wait in the dark, wanting

what they cannot want. Must we be given each
some curse? A face that furs and jowls at rising

moons? A body patchworked out of death?
In his greenhouse, the doctor tends rare molds

to reshape brains: the skull bones pliant as
music. We watch the Wolf change back into

a changeless man. He loves the nurse now:
her moonbeam white dresses. But Dracula

wants her, makes her play piano jazz riffs –
staccato, more staccato – with his eyes.

Despite ourselves, we understand that pull:
bone keys at midnight waiting for our hands,

the spirits waiting. Now even the doctor's mad:
vampiric blooded, stopping at nothing. What

cure remains? The house in flames. Everyone
so monstrous, so human.

ALEXANDRA TEAGUE (1974–)                                    57

*Years ago, a pregnant woman was bitten by a vampire*
*and turned. Her son was born with the thirst*
*but, being half human, he could walk in sunlight*
*unharmed. Though vampires quietly dominate the*
*world, he fights them — in part to prove his allegiance*
*to humanity, in part to avenge his long isolation, being*
*neither human, nor vampire. Because of his deadly*
*expertise and weapon of choice, they call him:*

BLADE, THE DAYWALKER

Like a stake
in my heart: this life —

the seen,
the unseen — the ones

who look in the mirror
and find nothing

but innocence though they stand
in blood up to their knees.

You see them: shadows
not shadows, people who seem

to be people. You don't
believe me? I watch

their news, drink coffee
in their chains.

There's no place
they haven't touched:

it's almost like I can't
wake up, like I'm living

in a movie, a kind of dream:
*action-packed thriller.*

I never
dreamed this

hunger in my veins, this
mind that cannot sleep: why

do I whet this blade,
when they will not die.

# BLADE, HISTORICAL

*It is possible that God exists, but with everything that has happened to us, could it possibly matter?*
— MARIO VARGAS LLOSA

You come into the world —
from where *from where* —
and the world turns

toward you, fangs bared,
disguised as what it is, as if
this is how it has to be:

as if it were normal to walk
the daylight knowing
something's wrong. *Grow up,*

they say, *get a job, go to church.*
And after awhile you stop
fighting it and try to smile.

Don't you ever wonder
whose blood is in
the banks? It's yours.

Follow the money
back to the Plague and
the rise of the papacy:

The Inquisition. The Burning
Times. The explorers
and the *explored*. So many

centuries, so much
death: you can still taste it
on the wind. Some days

I think, with the singing
of my blade, I can fix
everything – even the sadness

that says nothing that matters
will change. Some days
I think I should never have been.

TIM SEIBLES (1955–)                    61

# THE VAMPIRE

She rose among us where we lay.
She wept, we put our work away.
She chilled our laughter, stilled our play;
And spread a silence there.
And darkness shot across the sky,
And once, and twice, we heard her cry;
And saw her lift white hands on high
And toss her troubled hair.

What shape was this who came to us,
With basilisk eyes so ominous,
With mouth so sweet, so poisonous,
And tortured hands so pale?
We saw her wavering to and fro,
Through dark and wind we saw her go;
Yet what her name was did not know;
And felt our spirits fail.

We tried to turn away; but still
Above we heard her sorrow thrill;
And those that slept, they dreamed of ill
And dreadful things:
Of skies grown red with rending flames
And shuddering hills that cracked their frames;
Of twilights foul with wings;

And skeletons dancing to a tune;
And cries of children stifled soon;
And over all a blood-red moon
A dull and nightmare size.
They woke, and sought to go their ways,
Yet everywhere they met her gaze,
Her fixed and burning eyes.

Who are you now, – we cried to her –
Spirit so strange, so sinister?
We felt dead winds above us stir;
And in the darkness heard
A voice fall, singing, cloying sweet,
Heavily dropping, though that heat,
Heavy as honeyed pulses beat,
Slow word by anguished word.

And through the night strange music went
With voice and cry so darkly blent
We could not fathom what they meant;
Save only that they seemed
To thin the blood along our veins,
Foretelling vile, delirious pains,
And clouds divulging blood-red rains
Upon a hill undreamed.

And this we heard: "Who dies for me,
He shall possess me secretly,
My terrible beauty he shall see,
And slake my body's flame.
But who denies me cursed shall be,
And slain, and buried loathsomely,
And slimed upon with shame."

And darkness fell. And like a sea
Of stumbling deaths we followed, we
Who dared not stay behind.
There all night long beneath a cloud
We rose and fell, we struck and bowed,
We were the ploughman and the ploughed,
Our eyes were red and blind.

And some, they said, had touched her side,
Before she fled us there;
And some had taken her to bride;
And some lain down for her and died;
Who had not touched her hair,
Ran to and fro and cursed and cried
And sought her everywhere.

"Her eyes have feasted on the dead,
And small and shapely is her head,
And dark and small her mouth," they said,

"And beautiful to kiss;
Her mouth is sinister and red
As blood in moonlight is."

Then poets forgot their jeweled words
And cut the sky with glittering swords;
And innocent souls turned carrion birds
To perch upon the dead.
Sweet daisy fields were drenched with death,
The air became a charnel breath,
Pale stones were splashed with red.

Green leaves were dappled bright with blood
And fruit trees murdered in the bud;
And when at length the dawn
Came green as twilight from the east,
And all that heaving horror ceased,
Silent was every bird and beast,
And that dark voice was gone.

No word was there, no song, no bell,
No furious tongue that dream to tell;
Only the dead, who rose and fell
Above the wounded men;
And whisperings and wails of pain
Blown slowly from the wounded grain,
Blown slowly from the smoking plain;
And silence fallen again.

Until at dusk, from God knows where,
Beneath dark birds that filled the air,
Like one who did not hear or care,
Under a blood-red cloud,
An aged ploughman came alone
And drove his share through flesh and bone,
And turned them under to mould and stone;
All night long he ploughed.

# COUNT ORLOK

Mr. Barlow in the film of *Salem's Lot*
had been bitten by this old and silent grandsire
– bloated tick of a head, and the white stare
daring its meal to blink; the spirit fingers
long, on arms themselves too long
for the ghost torso, ending in sickle
fingernails which reap around the edges.
That same affectless banshee gaze, as if
shocked to think what struggles in a sack;
the haunted arms retracted, sick with hunger's
tightening suck inside the drainpipe chest,
the stealth alive and jerky on the sudden
though oddly stiff, owing to his need
to put not a wraith foot wrong in this gloom
infested with the sicknesses of rats.
He was a phantom limb that ached between
Bram Stoker and Lugosi, the flickering amputation,
his awkwardly edited, overacted
jump cuts on Murnau's screen
killed by the light but repeatedly brought to life
through remembering projections. His stark skull
fathering the dome of Giger's Alien,
stared down all the gorgeous Hammer vampires.
And the teeth. His crowded cutters
not the canines of well bred familiars,

but front incisors for a rodent
piercing, sank themselves
into the undercurrent of our bloodstream,
decanting hidden dreams since '22
gorged on *Ulysses*, *The Waste Land*, *Nosferatu*.

## MY CHILDHOOD NIGHTMARES
## UNFOLDED IN SERIAL NARRATIVE

"David, you don't want them to send
you away, do you," Carolyn says,

"to a home for mentally disturbed
children" – exactly what my father

used to tell me when I threw a tantrum
(my reply, stuffing temper fits inside,

gunpowder packed into a cannon bore,
known in the *DSM-IV* as Code 300.02,

"Generalized Anxiety Disorder").
Like a conventional soap opera

story arc – Dr. Hoffman planting
an unconscious suggestion in Vicki

to stay away from Barnabas, while
Barnabas in turn drinks Carolyn's

blood, enslaving her, commanding
that she bring Vicki to be his vampire

bride, the new Josette – my childhood
nightmares unfolded in a serial narrative,

three or four times per week, so often
I stopped waking my parents (how could

they, mortals, possibly protect me from
a vampire), and each night Barnabas

got closer, moving from front yard
to roof, then sliding down the shingles

to stare into my bedroom window.

# THE VIEW FROM HAROLD WAY

*for Bela Lugosi,*
*from his last address*

It's almost Palm Sunday
and so the palm fronds hang like razor blades
in honor of the season, cutting at the sky
as the canvas of the day
narrows its hues to black and white
and perhaps he wonders –
how does one rehearse a heart attack
after all those years of playing somebody
who doesn't get to die.

He moves from the southern window,
glancing at the wreck of corrugated tin
that lines the eaves
to the rambling house next door
where the paint is gradually
feathering into wind,
leaving wood as exposed and gray
as his own hair.

The rug holds years of someone else's cigarette burns
and the smells of other people's lives.
It is a shabby place to end
after all those cathedrals.

But below the eastern window,
a hint of the old spectral elegance
remains – the iron entry gate
is scrolled and resembles, he realizes,
the entrance to a cemetery –
the gray sidewalk stretching to the house
a flattened tombstone
or the grave of a giant
from whose bones
a grove of calla lilies
interrupts the dark,
the flowers' lips like widening, distended candles
spent from the heat of a firm wick
and cooling in the falling night

and as he imagines what it would be
to fly out this window
in the form of a bat, he gazes
down at the long sidewalk
and knows, after all, he's just a man
who looks, for a second,
up the suddenly steep hill beyond the gate,
a rising mound of gray,
where lit up for the night
and spelling the name of the cemetery
are those large white wooden letters:

HOLLYWOOD.

72  SARAH MACLAY (1956–)

# THE
# INCORPOREAL
# UNDEAD

## DEAD HOODLUMS

They go on holding up the street arcades
of the Paseo de Julio, vain
shades fighting always with their sister shades
or with the wolf of hunger – that other pain.
When sun diminishes into a star
yellowing borders of the slums, those lives
go back into their dusk, crepuscular,
lethal and dead, back to their whores and knives.
They live on in apocryphal tall stories,
in swagger and the strumming of a string,
and in a face, and in a whistling,
in things of poverty and in dark glories,
and in an inner grapevine-shadowed yard
when a hand is tuning a guitar.

JORGE LUIS BORGES (1899–1986)                    75
TRANS. TONY BARNSTONE

## GHOST TANGO

Two electricians argue in Russian
over how to run a line from a chandelier
to the dimming switch.

The one with long eyelashes asks
if he could play his CD on her stereo.

*Argentine Tango*, he says,
after the chandelier is hung,
the dimming switch tested.
*You like?*

She says, *I like*, and he offers
to teach the steps, puts his hand
on the small of her back, plants his eyes
on her breasts, braless beneath this flimsy
red blouse, tilts her steep until her curls
river the checkered tiles.

That night, she puts on a blue strapless gown,
invites in her dead lover's emaciated ghost.
He comes in through the window, takes her
in his bony moonbeam arms, and they tango
like two broken violins in love.

76   SHOLEH WOLPÉ (1962–)

## WORDS FOR SPRING

The boy in the boots comes galumphing.
Where he starts the yard, a hammock sags

with the ghost of Gramps pretending to snoozle,

don't bother me now, five more minutes.
In the crepe myrtle! Look!

Darn, too late – there go two cardinals,

flitting through doodles of light,
swooping, and redfull as

the springtime is short.

Muddy clay. The boy scrapes
bootbottoms on brick,

rubber scrubbed to green –

then dirty and delighted
and meteored with mud,

he draggles his sweatshirt into the kitchen,

slurs the clean linoleum,
sleevesmears his nose with snot.

Any cookies in the jar?

Just a crumbly and a nub.
The ghost of Gramps pours himself

the last glass of milk, too full.

He's just being spitty:
everyone knows that ghosts don't drink.

And the boy would drink the drink

if the mean ghost of Gramps
would put down the glass.

Won't he put down the glass?

If only the boy could bewilder
his own feet and hands,

he'd walk through the ghost thing,

reach for the cold shiny milk.
If only. Instead the boy will

will his thirst away

and deedle back out
into the leafshade of the porch,

so taken with nothing

doing nothing, out there on the lawn,
he'll turn to a bookdream, to be

joined by wheezy Gramps packing a pipe,

man and boy nodding
in their separate thoughts together,

one dead, the other alive.

# IN THE DUST

And then in the dust he drew a face,
the face of a woman, and he asked
the man drinking whiskey beside him
if he'd ever seen her, or knew who she was,
all the time staring down at her, as if
this would make her whole. And then,
at the shake of the head, he let his boot
dissolve her into a settling cloud.
He threw another plank on the fire,
drained his glass and filled it again,
watching his dog rise to its feet
and start to growl at the dirt road
that stretched, empty, to a hilly horizon.
A shiver coincided with the dog's first bark,
that doubled, trebled, became gunfire
that stopped nothing coming, so he stood
to confront it, but not even a wind
brushed his face, no shape formed,
and after the dog went quiet, a hand
helped him sit down and rejoin his glass.

## THE AFTERLIFE: LETTER
## TO SAM HAMILL

You may think it strange, Sam, that I'm writing
a letter in these circumstances. I thought
it strange too – the first time. But there's
a misconception I was laboring under, and you
are too, viz. that the imagination in your
vicinity is free and powerful. After all,
you say, you've been creating yourself all
along imaginatively. You imagine yourself
playing golf or hiking in the Olympics or
writing a poem and then it becomes true.
But you still have to do it, you have to exert
yourself, will, courage, whatever you've got, you're
mired in the unimaginative. Here I imagine a letter
and it's written. Takes about two-fifths of a
second, your time. Hell, this is heaven, man.
I can deluge Congress with letters telling
every one of those mendacious sons of bitches
exactly what he or she is, in maybe about
half an hour. In spite of your Buddhist
proclivities, when you imagine bliss
you still must struggle to get there. By the way
the Buddha has his place across town on
Elysian Drive. We call him Bud. He's lost weight
and got new dentures, and he looks a hell of a

lot better than he used to. He always carries
a jumping jack with him everywhere just
for contemplation, but he doesn't make it
jump. He only looks at it. Meanwhile Sidney
and Dizzy, Uncle Ben and Papa Yancey, are
over by Sylvester's Grot making the sweetest,
cheerfulest blues you ever heard. The air,
so called, is full of it. Poems are fluttering
everywhere like seed from a cottonwood tree.
Sam, the remarkable truth is I can do any
fucking thing I want. Speaking of which
there's this dazzling young Naomi who
wiped out on I-80 just west of Truckee
last winter, and I think this is the moment
for me to go and pay her my respects.
Don't go way. I'll be right back.

# NOCTURNE

That scraping of iron on iron when the wind
rises, what is it? Something the wind won't
quit with, but drags back and forth.
Sometimes faint, far, then suddenly, close, just
beyond the screened door, as if someone there
squats in the dark honing his wares against
my threshold. Half steel wire, half metal wing,
nothing and anything might make this noise
of saws and rasps, a creaking and groaning
of bone-growth, or body-death, marriages of rust,
or ore abraded. Tonight, something bows
that should not bend. Something stiffens that should
slide. Something, loose and not right,
rakes or forges itself all night.

LI-YOUNG LEE (1957)

# WE ARE SEVEN

———A simple Child,
That lightly draws its breath,
And feels its life in every limb,
What should it know of death?

I met a little cottage Girl:
She was eight years old, she said;
Her hair was thick with many a curl
That clustered round her head.

She had a rustic, woodland air,
And she was wildly clad:
Her eyes were fair, and very fair;
– Her beauty made me glad.

"Sisters and brothers, little Maid,
How many may you be?"
"How many? Seven in all," she said,
And wondering looked at me.

"And where are they? I pray you tell."
She answered, "Seven are we;
And two of us at Conway dwell,
And two are gone to sea.

"Two of us in the church-yard lie,
My sister and my brother;
And, in the church-yard cottage, I
Dwell near them with my mother."

"You say that two at Conway dwell,
And two are gone to sea,
Yet ye are seven! I pray you tell,
Sweet Maid, how this may be."

Then did the little Maid reply,
"Seven boys and girls are we;
Two of us in the church-yard lie,
Beneath the church-yard tree."

"You run about, my little Maid,
Your limbs they are alive;
If two are in the church-yard laid,
Then ye are only five."

"Their graves are green, they may be seen,"
The little Maid replied,
"Twelve steps or more from my mother's door,
And they are side by side.

"My stockings there I often knit,
My kerchief there I hem;
And there upon the ground I sit,
And sing a song to them.

"And often after sunset, Sir,
When it is light and fair,
I take my little porringer,
And eat my supper there.

"The first that died was sister Jane;
In bed she moaning lay,
Till God released her of her pain;
And then she went away.

"So in the church-yard she was laid;
And, when the grass was dry,
Together round her grave we played,
My brother John and I.

"And when the ground was white with snow,
And I could run and slide,
My brother John was forced to go,
And he lies by her side."

"How many are you, then," said I,
"If they two are in heaven?"
Quick was the little Maid's reply,
"O Master! we are seven."

"But they are dead; those two are dead!
Their spirits are in heaven!"
'Twas throwing words away; for still
The little Maid would have her will,
And said, "Nay, we are seven!"

# I LAST SAW MY MOTHER

I last saw my mother a week after her suicide, in a
dream. She was so shy; she was only there a moment.
I'd called her stupid. How could you be so stupid?
Eight years later she's back. What do you want, I ask
her, what do you really want? I want to sing, she says.
And she sings.

## NO. 670 (ONE NEED NOT BE A CHAMBER – TO BE HAUNTED)

One need not be a Chamber – to be Haunted –
One need not be a House –
The Brain has Corridors – surpassing
Material Place –

Far safer, of a Midnight Meeting
External Ghost
Than its interior Confronting –
That Cooler Host.

Far safer, through an Abbey gallop,
The Stones a'chase –
Than Unarmed, one's a'self encounter –
In lonesome Place –

Ourself behind ourself, concealed –
Should startle most –
Assassin hid in our Apartment
Be Horror's least.

The Body – borrows a Revolver –
He bolts the Door –
O'erlooking a superior spectre –
Or More –

EMILY DICKINSON (1830–86)

# HAUNTED

"Mom Hosts Haunted House In Home Where
Children Died."

— KTLA NEWS

Called here as if by telepathy, the crowd
adores the giant: nine feet tall; huge, curled
fingers gouging the ground. He lunges;
we scream, leap back like stomped water,
then slosh forward as he blomps away.

"How'd they do this?" parents say,
meaning make the house look authentically
burned: charred boards, collapsed roof,
floors black as eggs forgotten on the stove.
The man who, as he chats with guests,

melts into a skeleton, looks real. So does
the corpse who smiles on his autopsy-
table, organs shimmery with worms.
Zombie-heads with hot-coal eyes
surprise two teenaged girls, who stampede

with ecstatic shrieks beneath the Green-
Glow EXIT sign. Plunging
through webs twitchy with tarantulas,
they burst outside, where a witch clunks
Milky Ways into their sacks, a warty

mask hiding the face that, just last year,
was hideous with helplessness
to save her little boys when their heater –
bought to keep them snug – lit
the drapes she'd hung to help them sleep.

Only the neighbors know why two small
gravestones hog the whole front yard,
and why the actor in the giant-suit
takes care, in his stilt-high stumblings, not
to knock them down.

# GHOST HOUSE

I dwell in a lonely house I know
That vanished many a summer ago,
 And left no trace but the cellar walls,
 And a cellar in which the daylight falls
And the purple-stemmed wild raspberries grow.

O'er ruined fences the grape-vines shield
The woods come back to the mowing field;
 The orchard tree has grown one copse
 Of new wood and old where the woodpecker chops;
The footpath down to the well is healed.

I dwell with a strangely aching heart
In that vanished abode there far apart
 On that disused and forgotten road
 That has no dust-bath now for the toad.
Night comes; the black bats tumble and dart;

The whippoorwill is coming to shout
And hush and cluck and flutter about:
 I hear him begin far enough away
 Full many a time to say his say
Before he arrives to say it out.

It is under the small, dim, summer star.
I know not who these mute folk are
    Who share the unlit place with me –
    Those stones out under the low-limbed tree
Doubtless bear names that the mosses mar.

They are tireless folk, but slow and sad –
Though two, close-keeping, are lass and lad –
    With none among them that ever sings,
    And yet, in view of how many things,
As sweet companions as might be had.

DANIEL

On the day we moved in, the pings, bumps, and snaps
Were scary, it's true, but probably normal;
A house accepting new patterns of weight
With protest, the way no conviction goes gently.
We laughed a little, and called it "our spirit."

Later that night, when the power conked out
And the kids were crying, the ghost got a name,
"Daniel," and a history of whispered exploits,
All of them harmless, like nursery rhymes,
Or like the little fibs we tell ourselves
To explain why this or that has led to suffering.

Pretty soon, we were using him for everything.
When the Christmas tree fell, it was "Daniel";
When my wife lost her ring, it was "Daniel";
When the kids forgot to feed the goldfish
And it turned up dead, its eyes silvered over
Like water shadowed under sheets of ice,

Well, that became Daniel too, which was curious;
And pauses me now as I make the long walk
Down the hall to the bathroom in darkness,
And hear, in soft concert, the sound of my footfalls
Answered at once by my children's voices

Still calling to Daniel behind their door.

## *From* LITTLE GIDDING

### II

Ash on an old man's sleeve
Is all the ash the burnt roses leave.
Dust in the air suspended
Marks the place where a story ended.
Dust inbreathed was a house –
The wall, the wainscot and the mouse.
The death of hope and despair,
      This is the death of air.

There are flood and drouth
Over the eyes and in the mouth,
Dead water and dead sand
Contending for the upper hand.
The parched eviscerate soil
Gapes at the vanity of toil,
Laughs without mirth.
      This is the death of earth.

Water and fire succeed
The town, the pasture and the weed.
Water and fire deride
The sacrifice that we denied.
Water and fire shall rot
The marred foundations we forgot,
Of sanctuary and choir.
      This is the death of water and fire.

In the uncertain hour before the morning
    Near the ending of interminable night
    At the recurrent end of the unending
After the dark dove with the flickering tongue
    Had passed below the horizon of his homing
    While the dead leaves still rattled on like tin
Over the asphalt where no other sound was
    Between three districts whence the smoke arose
    I met one walking, loitering and hurried
As if blown towards me like the metal leaves
    Before the urban dawn wind unresisting.
    And as I fixed upon the down-turned face
That pointed scrutiny with which we challenge
    The first-met stranger in the waning dusk
    I caught the sudden look of some dead master
Whom I had known, forgotten, half recalled
    Both one and many; in the brown baked features
    The eyes of a familiar compound ghost
Both intimate and unidentifiable.
    So I assumed a double part, and cried
    And heard another's voice cry: "What! are *you*
        here?"
Although we were not. I was still the same,
    Knowing myself yet being someone other –
    And he a face still forming; yet the words sufficed
To compel the recognition they preceded.
    And so, compliant to the common wind,

Too strange to each other for misunderstanding,
In concord at this intersection time
   Of meeting nowhere, no before and after,
   We trod the pavement in a dead patrol.
I said: "The wonder that I feel is easy,
   Yet ease is cause of wonder. Therefore speak:
   I may not comprehend, may not remember."
And he: "I am not eager to rehearse
   My thoughts and theory which you have forgotten.
   These things have served their purpose: let them be.
So with your own, and pray they be forgiven
   By others, as I pray you to forgive
   Both bad and good. Last season's fruit is eaten
And the fullfed beast shall kick the empty pail.
   For last year's words belong to last year's language
   And next year's words await another voice.
But, as the passage now presents no hindrance
   To the spirit unappeased and peregrine
   Between two worlds become much like each other,
So I find words I never thought to speak
   In streets I never thought I should revisit
   When I left my body on a distant shore.
Since our concern was speech, and speech impelled us
   To purify the dialect of the tribe
   And urge the mind to aftersight and foresight,
Let me disclose the gifts reserved for age
   To set a crown upon your lifetime's effort.

First, the cold friction of expiring sense
Without enchantment, offering no promise
But bitter tastelessness of shadow fruit
As body and soul begin to fall asunder.
Second, the conscious impotence of rage
At human folly, and the laceration
Of laughter at what ceases to amuse.
And last, the rending pain of re-enactment
Of all that you have done, and been; the shame
Of motives late revealed, and the awareness
Of things ill done and done to others' harm
Which once you took for exercise of virtue.
Then fools' approval stings, and honour stains.
From wrong to wrong the exasperated spirit
Proceeds, unless restored by that refining fire
Where you must move in measure, like a dancer."
The day was breaking. In the disfigured street
He left me, with a kind of valediction,
And faded on the blowing of the horn.

# PAINT

*White,* he said, *I'm going to paint everything white. Good,*
she said, *It's about time, it's time to paint everything white.*
*Yes,* he said. And he pulled out a large brush and
painted the words *everything* and *white* on the wall in a
very attractive hand, words which happened to be the
first two of the novel he'd just begun writing of the
same name. She was not amused. *I'm not amused,* she
said. *Paint, this place is filthy.* He painted the words *was
kept in a separate room* across the wall and onto the
window, then *until the snow fell and it was taken outside
which is when they met . . .* and on and on until the walls
were filled and the floor, the chapters becoming
indistinguishable. She said, *The place looks great, you're
a good painter. Thanks,* he said, and he took off his
clothes to begin the last chapter on his legs. It was a
love story, but also a mystery because it turns out the
two lovers had been dead all along. *Dead people can't be
characters,* she said, *It's not right.* And she took off her
shirt and pants and said, *Paint, it can't end like this.*
Of course, it could end any way he wanted, so he
kissed her as he painted *yes* over and over until she
disappeared.

# THE SHADOW ON THE STONE

I went by the Druid stone
That broods in the garden white and lone,
And I stopped and looked at the shifting shadows
That at some moments fall thereon
From the tree hard by with a rhythmic swing,
And they shaped in my imagining
To the shade that a well-known head and shoulders
Threw there when she was gardening.

I thought her behind my back,
Yea, her I long had learned to lack,
And I said: "I am sure you are standing behind me.
Though how do you get into this old track?"
And there was no sound but the fall of a leaf
As a sad response; and to keep down grief
I would not turn my head to discover
That there was nothing in my belief.

Yet I wanted to look and see
That nobody stood at the back of me;
But I thought once more: "Nay, I'll not unvision
A shape which, somehow, there may be."
So I went on softly from the glade,
And left her behind me throwing her shade,
As she were indeed an apparition –
My head unturned lest my dream should fade.

# GOODBYE TO A POLTERGEIST

Like an empty socket alone
On a long baseboard, nothing connects
With him anymore. The bundled family
Has tramped away with its suitcases.
In the spots where he hid he finds light.
To him the dust, with nothing to settle on,
Is a dreary rain.

His push-and-pull with the household gods
Is over; his own knocking rattles him.
His squatter's rights continue but how
To assert them with no one living to gibber at,
No sleeping ear to enter
Or hot brain to poach his eye, the nightmare?

Perhaps, he never existed.
Perhaps, with new residents he will find himself
No longer himself; some unfamiliar dampness
Under a bed will expel him,
A fresh draft blow him deep between floorboards.
He is slowly unfolding, like a crumpled paper
Left in a closet, inanimately with a faint creak.

He needs the children who lived here, who are now
Releasing rolls of streamers from a boatside.
What a mess of tape as the bright wheels unspin
And the boat is tugged out.
In their minds, his rooms, his house, his drizzle of dust
In the cleansing light are cut to ribbons
And sink like ribbons, absorbed by the air.

# I ONLY AM ESCAPED ALONE
## TO TELL THEE

I tell you that I see her still
At the dark entrance of the hall.
One gas lamp burning near her shoulder
Shone also from her other side
Where hung the long inaccurate glass
Whose pictures were as troubled water.
An immense shadow had its hand
Between us on the floor, and seemed
To hump the knuckles nervously,
A giant crab readying to walk,
Or a blanket moving in its sleep.

You will remember, with a smile
Instructed by movies to reminisce,
How strict her corsets must have been,
How the huge arrangements of her hair
Would certainly betray the least
Impassionate displacement there.
It was no rig for dallying,
And maybe only marriage could
Derange that queenly scaffolding –
As when a great ship, coming home,
Coasts in the harbor, dropping sail
And loosing all the tackle that had laced

Her in the long lanes....
                    I know
We need not draw this figure out.
But all that whalebone came from whales.
And all the whales lived in the sea,
In calm beneath the troubled glass,
Until the needle drew their blood.

I see her standing in the hall,
Where the mirror's lashed to blood and foam,
And the black flukes of agony
Beat at the air till the light blows out.

# THE GHOST OF KING HAMLET
(*From Hamlet*)

I am thy father's spirit,
Doom'd for a certain term to walk the night,
And for the day confin'd to fast in fires,
Till the foul crimes done in my days of nature
Are burnt and purg'd away. But that I am forbid
To tell the secrets of my prison-house,
I could a tale unfold whose lightest word
Would harrow up thy soul, freeze thy young blood,
Make thy two eyes, like stars, start from their spheres,
Thy knotted and combined locks to part,
And each particular hair to stand on end,
Like quills upon the fretful porpentine.
But this eternal blazon must not be
To ears of flesh and blood. List, list, O, list!
If thou didst ever thy dear father love [...]
Revenge his foul and most unnatural murder [...]
Murder most foul, as in the best it is;
But this most foul, strange, and unnatural [...]
                              I find thee apt;
And duller shouldst thou be than the fat weed
That roots itself in ease on Lethe wharf,
Wouldst thou not stir in this. Now, Hamlet, hear:
'Tis given out that, sleeping in my orchard,
A serpent stung me; so the whole ear of Denmark

Is by a forged process of my death
Rankly abus'd; but know, thou noble youth,
The serpent that did sting thy father's life
Now wears his crown [...]
Ay, that incestuous, that adulterate beast,
With witchcraft of his wits, with traitorous gifts –
O wicked wit and gifts that have the power
So to seduce! – won to his shameful lust
The will of my most seeming virtuous queen.
O Hamlet, what a falling off was there,
From me, whose love was of that dignity
That it went hand in hand even with the vow
I made to her in marriage; and to decline
Upon a wretch whose natural gifts were poor
To those of mine!
But virtue, as it never will be moved,
Though lewdness court it in a shape of heaven,
So lust, though to a radiant angel link'd,
Will sate itself in a celestial bed
And prey on garbage.
But, soft! methinks I scent the morning air.
Brief let me be. Sleeping within my orchard,
My custom always of the afternoon,
Upon my secure hour thy uncle stole,
With juice of cursed hebena in a vial,
And in the porches of my ears did pour
The leperous distilment; whose effect

Holds such an enmity with blood of man
That swift as quicksilver it courses through
The natural gates and alleys of the body;
And with a sudden vigour it doth posset
And curd, like eager droppings into milk,
The thin and wholesome blood. So did it mine;
And a most instant tetter bark'd about,
Most lazar-like, with vile and loathsome crust,
All my smooth body.
Thus was I, sleeping, by a brother's hand
Of life, of crown, of queen, at once dispatch'd:
Cut off even in the blossoms of my sin,
Unhous'led, disappointed, unanel'd,
No reck'ning made, but sent to my account
With all my imperfections on my head:
O, horrible! O, horrible! most horrible!
If thou hast nature in thee, bear it not;
Let not the royal bed of Denmark be
A couch for luxury and damned incest.
But, howsoever thou pursuest this act,
Taint not thy mind, nor let thy soul contrive
Against thy mother aught; leave her to heaven
And to those thorns that in her bosom lodge
To prick and sting her. Fare thee well at once.
The glow-worm shows the matin to be near,
And 'gins to pale his uneffectual fire.
Adieu, adieu, adieu! Remember me.

WILLIAM SHAKESPEARE (1564–1616)          107

# LABUNTUR ET IMPUTANTUR

It was overcast. No hour at all was indicated by the
    gnomon.
With difficulty I made out the slogan, *Time and tide*
    *wait for no man.*

I had been waiting for you, Daphne, underneath the
    dripping laurels, near
The sundial glade where first we met. I felt like
    Hamlet on the parapets of Elsinore,

Alerted to the ectoplasmic moment, when Luna rends
    her shroud of cloud
And sails into a starry archipelago. Then your
    revenant appeared and spake aloud:

*I am not who you think I am. For what we used to be is*
    *gone. The moment's over,*
*Whatever years you thought we spent together. You don't*
    *know the story. And moreover,*

*You mistook the drinking-fountain for a sundial.* I put my
    lips to its whatever,
And with difficulty I made out the slogan, *Drink from*
    *me and you shall live forever.*

# VOICES FROM THE OTHER WORLD

Presently at our touch the teacup stirred,
Then circled lazily about
From A to Z. The first voice heard
(If they are voices, these mute spellers-out)
Was that of an engineer

Originally from Cologne.
Dead in his 22nd year
Of cholera in Cairo, he had KNOWN
NO HAPPINESS. He once met Goethe, though.
Goethe had told him: PERSEVERE.

Our blind hound whined. With that, a horde
Of voices gathered above the Ouija board,
Some childish and, you might say, blurred
By sleep; one little boy
Named Will, reluctant possibly in a ruff

Like a large-lidded page out of El Greco, pulled
Back the arras for that next voice,
Cold and portentous: ALL IS LOST.
FLEE THIS HOUSE. OTTO VON THURN
    UND TAXIS.
OBEY. YOU HAVE NO CHOICE.

Frightened, we stopped; but tossed
Till sunrise striped the rumpled sheets with gold.
Each night since then, the moon waxes,
Small insects flit round a cold torch
We light, that sends them pattering to the porch ...

But no real Sign. New voices come,
Dictate addresses, begging us to write;
Some warn of lives misspent, and all of doom
In ways that so exhilarate
We are sleeping sound of late.

Last night the teacup shattered in a rage.
Indeed, we have grown nonchalant
Towards the other world. In the gloom here,
Our elbows on the cleared
Table, we talk and smoke, pleased to be stirred

Rather by buzzings in the jasmine, by the drone
Of our own voices and poor blind Rover's wheeze,
Than by those clamoring overhead,
Obsessed or piteous, for a commitment
We still have wit to postpone

Because, once looked at lit
By the cold reflections of the dead
Risen extinct but irresistible,
Our lives have never seemed more full, more real,
Nor the full moon more quick to chill.

110   JAMES MERRILL (1926–95)

*From* THE INVISIBLE

The moment you shut off the lamp,
Here they are again,
The two dead people
You called your parents.

You'd hoped you'd see tonight
The girl you loved once,
And that other one who let you
Slip a hand under her skirt.

Instead, here's that key in a saucer of small change
That wouldn't open any lock,
The used condom you found in church,
The lame crow your neighbor kept.

Here's the fly you once tortured,
A rock you threw at your best friend,
The pig that let out a scream
As the knife touched its throat.

## GHOSTS

Some ghosts are women,
neither abstract nor pale,
their breasts as limp as killed fish.
Not witches, but ghosts
who come, moving their useless arms
like forsaken servants.

Not all ghosts are women,
I have seen others;
fat, white-bellied men,
wearing their genitals like old rags.
Not devils, but ghosts.
This one thumps barefoot, lurching
above my bed.

But that isn't all.
Some ghosts are children.
Not angels, but ghosts;
curling like pink tea cups
on any pillow, or kicking,
showing their innocent bottoms, wailing
for Lucifer.

# GHOST

I felt soft fingers at my throat
It seemed someone was strangling me

The lips were hard as they were sweet
It seemed someone was kissing me

My vital bones about to crack
I gaped into another's eyes

I saw it was a face I knew
A face as sweet as it was grim

It did not smile it did not weep
Its eyes were wide and white its skin

I did not smile I did not weep
I raised my hand and touched its cheek

HAROLD PINTER (1930–2008)                    113

# THE WHITE GHOSTS

White ghosts were ruining the neighborhood
like an army of blank real estate signs,
like refrigerators abandoned on front lawns
that were really graveyards.
This occurred to me while I took a shower
with the sister of my former wife.
She was so afraid of the white ghosts,
she wore her bathing suit
and over that, her dark blue dress.
I wrote this down on her dress
with a pen that had white, waterproof ink.
I wanted to write more about the white ghosts
so I peeled her dress off.
She liked that and kissed me,
sticking her tongue into my mouth.
Her tongue was not soft and warm
but stiff and cool like cardboard,
and tasted like a communion wafer.
Then I lay next to you thinking,
it's good I brought her dress with me
so I could write about the white ghosts.
Then I thought, you fool, you can't carry
things out of a dream, so forget about
the white ghosts. I got up and took
my dog to the park but he would not

get out of the car. I don't know for sure,
but I think the field was full of white ghosts,
and he could see them standing there,
silent, like the ghosts of a Ku Klux Klan meeting.
White noise is not white.
White chocolate is not chocolate.
Avalanches are not soft and fluffy.
When I got home, the ghost
of a white pit bull was writhing
on the kitchen floor, whining and sliding
toward me across the linoleum on her belly.

## HOTEL WINDOW

Aura of absence, vertigo of non-being –
could I ever express what happened?
It was nothing, really, or next to nothing.

I was standing at the window at dusk
watching the cabs or the ghosts of cabs
lining up on the other side of the street

like yellow ferryboats waiting to cross
a great divide. All afternoon the doorman
whistled through the shadows, Charon

slamming doors and shouting orders
at traffic piling up along the curb.
People got into cars and disappeared –

ordinary people, tourists, businessmen –
while fog thickened the city's features
and emptied out the color. I don't know

how long I stood there as darkness
inhabited air itself, but suddenly,
when it happened, everything seemed dis-

jointed, charged with non-existence,
as if a vast, drowned lake was rising
invisibly – permanently – from the ground.

At the same time nothing really changed,
footsteps still echoed in the hallway
and laughter flared up the stairwell,

the passengers flinging themselves into cabs
never noticed they were setting forth
on a voyage away from their bodies.

I felt within a sickening emptiness –
intangible, unruly – and I remember
lying down on the floor of the room ...

Then the phone rang and it was over.
Nothing happened – it took only a moment –
and it was dizzying, relentless, eternal.

EDWARD HIRSCH (1950–)    117

# THE APPARITION

When by thy scorn, O murderess, I am dead
    And that thou think'st thee free
From all solicitation from me,
Then shall my ghost come to thy bed,
And thee, feigned vestal, in worse arms shall see;
Then thy sick taper will begin to wink,
And he, whose thou art then, being tired before,
Will, if thou stir, or pinch to wake him, think
    Thou call'st for more,
And in false sleep will from thee shrink;
And then, poor aspen wretch, neglected thou
Bathed in a cold quicksilver sweat wilt lie
    A verier ghost than I.
What I will say, I will not tell thee now,
Lest that preserve thee; and since my love is spent,
I had rather thou shouldst painfully repent,
Than by my threatenings rest still innocent.

# GAS-LAMP GHOST

Out of the blue-gray dusk
He comes –
The ghostly one,
The gray one,
Driving his ghostly wagon.
Nearer he comes, and nearer,
Silent
Except for his singing flower
That burns a violet hole in the air,
That melts a violet hole in the snowy dusk.

He comes with a flower of burning mist
On the tip of a copper stalk;
He comes with a misty flower that sings
And burns a violet hole
In the blue-gray dusk.

He touches dark stems in a row,
He tips them with his hot mist-flower,
Stem after stem;
And one by one
They bloom, and glow,
And have white flowers on them,
And burn pale blue holes, green ghastly holes,

In the silent air,
In the blue-gray snowy dusk

RICHARD HUNT
(LATE 19TH–EARLY 20TH CENTURY)

# AS IF A PHANTOM CARESS'D ME

As if a phantom caress'd me,
I thought I was not alone walking here by the shore;
But the one I thought was with me as now I walk by
     the shore, the one I loved that caress'd me,
As I lean and look through the glimmering light, that
     one has utterly disappear'd,
And those appear that are hateful to me and mock me.

# THE INHERITANCE

Since you did depart
Out of my reach, my darling,
Into the hidden,
I see each shadow start
With recognition, and I
Am wonder-ridden.

I am dazed with the farewell,
But I scarcely feel your loss.
You left me a gift
Of tongués, so the shadows tell
Me things, and silences toss
Me their drift.

You sent me a cloven fire
Out of death, and it burns in the draught
Of the breathing hosts,
Kindles the darkening pyre
For the sorrowful, till strange brands waft
Like candid ghosts.

Form after form, in the streets
Waves like a ghost along,
Kindled to me;
The star above the house-top greets
Me every eve with a long
Song fierily.

All day long, the town
Glimmers with subtle ghosts
Going up and down
In a common, prison-like dress;
But their daunted looking flickers
To me, and I answer, Yes!

So I am not lonely nor sad
Although bereaved of you,
My little love.
I move among a kinsfolk clad
With words, but the dream shows through
As they move.

# THE UNQUIET GRAVE

"The wind doth blow today, my love,
And a few small drops of rain;
I never had but one true-love,
In cold grave she was lain.

"I'll do as much for my true-love
As any young man may;
I'll sit and mourn all at her grave
For a twelvemonth and a day."

The twelvemonth and a day being up,
The dead began to speak:
"Oh who sits weeping on my grave,
And will not let me sleep?"

"'Tis I, my love, sits on your grave,
And will not let you sleep;
For I crave one kiss of your clay-cold lips,
And that is all I seek."

"You crave one kiss of my clay-cold lips;
But my breath smells earthy strong;
If you have one kiss of my clay-cold lips,
Your time will not be long.

" 'Tis down in yonder garden green,
Love, where we used to walk,
The finest flower that ere was seen
Is withered to a stalk.

"The stalk is withered dry, my love,
So will our hearts decay;
So make yourself content, my love,
Till God calls you away."

# SONNET 23: METHOUGHT I SAW MY LATE ESPOUSED SAINT

Methought I saw my late espoused saint
 Brought to me like Alcestis from the grave,
 Whom Jove's great son to her glad husband gave,
Rescu'd from death by force, though pale and faint.
Mine, as whom wash'd from spot of child-bed taint
 Purification in the old Law did save,
 And such as yet once more I trust to have
 Full sight of her in Heaven without restraint,
Came vested all in white, pure as her mind.
 Her face was veil'd, yet to my fancied sight
 Love, sweetness, goodness in her person shin'd
So clear as in no face with more delight.
 But O as to embrace me she inclin'd,
 I wak'd, she fled, and day brought back my night.

JOHN MILTON (1608–74)

## (WEATHERVANE) PIRATE SHIP
## OF THE DEAD

It collected no more dust
Than was fashionable.
No more than when I used to wait
For the school bus across the street
Back when I stole everything.

Too many times it slashed
The milk of god's eye
In search of the old coves that
Huddle at the sky's curve.

Too robust of sail and pronounced
As fearless, it went on
In begging for its twin black crosses to be touched,
Its sea monster nose jutting out
And curling back to batter
The breast of an iron morning.

Now I won't refuse my place
In the painting that it proposes.
Now I won't tell
The perilous slope of roof
It forever swims above
A lie about my parting with thieves.

# BLUE DEMENTIA

In the days when a man
would hold a swarm of words
inside his belly, nestled
against his spleen, singing.

In the days of night riders
when life tongued a reed
till blues & sorrow song
called out of the deep night:
Another man done gone.
Another man done gone.

In the days when one could lose oneself
all up inside love that way,
& then moan on the bone
till the gods cried out in someone's sleep.

Today,
already I've seen three dark-skinned men
discussing the weather with demons
& angels, gazing up at the clouds
& squinting down into iron grates
along the fast streets of luminous encounters.

I double-check my reflection in plate glass
& wonder, Am I passing another
Lucky Thompson or Marion Brown
cornered by a blue dementia,
another dark-skinned man
who woke up dreaming one morning
& then walked out of himself
dreaming? Did this one dare
to step on a crack in the sidewalk,
to turn a midnight corner & never come back
whole, or did he try to stare down a look
that shoved a blade into his heart?
I mean, I also know something
about night riders & catgut. Yeah,
honey, I know something about talking with ghosts.

## THE GHOSTS
(*From The Song of Hiawatha*)

THE GHOSTS

Once at midnight Hiawatha,
Ever wakeful, ever watchful,
In the wigwam, dimly lighted
By the brands that still were burning,
By the glimmering, flickering firelight,
Heard a sighing, oft repeated,
Heard a sobbing, as of sorrow.

From his couch rose Hiawatha,
From his shaggy hides of bison,
Pushed aside the deer-skin curtain,
Saw the pallid guests, the shadows,
Sitting upright on their couches,
Weeping in the silent midnight.

And he said: "O guests! why is it
That your hearts are so afflicted,
That you sob so in the midnight?
Has perchance the old Nokomis,
Has my wife, my Minnehaha,
Wronged or grieved you by unkindness,
Failed in hospitable duties?"

Then the shadows ceased from weeping,
Ceased from sobbing and lamenting,
And they said, with gentle voices:
"We are ghosts of the departed,
Souls of those who once were with you.

From the realms of Chibiabos
Hither have we come to try you,
Hither have we come to warn you.

"Cries of grief and lamentation
Reach us in the Blessed Islands;
Cries of anguish from the living,
Calling back their friends departed,
Sadden us with useless sorrow.
Therefore have we come to try you;
No one knows us, no one heeds us.
We are but a burden to you,
And we see that the departed
Have no place among the living.

"Think of this, O Hiawatha!
Speak of it to all the people,
That henceforward and forever
They no more with lamentations
Sadden the souls of the departed
In the Islands of the Blessed.

"Do not lay such heavy burdens
In the graves of those you bury,
Not such weight of furs and wampum,
Not such weight of pots and kettles,
For the spirits faint beneath them.
Only give them food to carry,
Only give them fire to light them.

"Four days is the spirit's journey
To the land of ghosts and shadows,

130

Four its lonely night encampments;
Four times must their fires be lighted.
Therefore, when the dead are buried,
Let a fire, as night approaches,
Four times on the grave be kindled,
That the soul upon its journey
May not lack the cheerful firelight,
May not grope about in darkness.

"Farewell, noble Hiawatha!
We have put you to the trial,
To the proof have put your patience,
By the insult of our presence,
By the outrage of our actions.
We have found you great and noble.
Fail not in the greater trial,
Faint not in the harder struggle."

When they ceased, a sudden darkness
Fell and filled the silent wigwam.
Hiawatha heard a rustle
As of garments trailing by him,
Heard the curtain of the doorway
Lifted by a hand he saw not,
Felt the cold breath of the night air,
For a moment saw the starlight;
But he saw the ghosts no longer,
Saw no more the wandering spirits
From the kingdom of Ponemah,
From the land of the Hereafter.

# GREAT-GRANDMOTHER'S
# YOUNG GHOST

*H* er rocking chair sails the living room:
*E* ternity makes sense when the runners rock,
*R* iding the blue braided rug as a flume,
*R* ocking a sea of floorboards pocked
*O* ver and over by heels of a century
*C* arving their emphasis into the floors,
*K* nocking the years into waves that now crash
*I* nto shores – the oaken arms the oak of oars.
*N* othing can be put behind her fury
*G* rinding the waves. How far from the wall her
*C* hair must be battened – its slender shape, like
*H* er hair, flings wildly as it rocks, all
*A* ir bestirred. If you try her chair, life crashes
*I* ts way through the frumious
*R* olling as if, through you, she's there.

# IN ORDER TO TALK WITH THE DEAD

In order to talk with the dead
you have to choose words
that they recognize as easily
as their hands
recognized the fur of their dogs in the dark.
Words clear and calm
as water of the torrent tamed in the wineglass
or chairs the mother puts in order
after the guests have left.
Words that night shelters
as marshes do their ghostly fires.

In order to talk with the dead
you have to know how to wait:
they are fearful
like the first steps of a child.
But if we are patient
one day they will answer us
with a poplar leaf trapped in a broken mirror,
with a flame that suddenly revives in the fireplace,
with a dark return of birds
before the glance of a girl
who waits motionless on the threshold.

JORGE TEILLIER (1935–96)                    133
TRANS. CAROLYNE WRIGHT

# THE PANTHER

"Walking the gravel driveway
to retrieve the daily mail, a whisper surged
through the grassy field. I stopped for a long
moment – flexed, alert.
Isobars of pressure rippled my shirt
against my breasts. The world seemed
a test, as in a Borges story – the answer,
*ghost*, at the corner of my eye.

Once, through the front window
I watched my daughter draw sun circles
on scrap wood alongside the grain bin.
She came still, slowly tilted
her head toward the field.
I felt the call in my body
to save her, but I held.
I wanted so badly to see
what might emerge from wheat shade
into real day. Nothing. Nothing ever.

The worst of it's at night
when I wake from a dream of tangled
bodies, in love with a dead man,
to sense beyond uncertainty
the gaze upon my body.

Still, careful, I open
my eyes and find her at the bedside
whispering into dream space.
Sinuous, almost feline, she evades and I
lie alone listening through this
cloud world for breathing to surround.

Finally entirely undone
I told the man who brought our firewood:
*Something watches us.*
*I can't trust my mind.*
Out of kind curiosity, he installed cameras
like the ones he used for hunting.
I felt certain nothing visible would register.

She would be five that summer.
She and I, the survived. Alone. Alive.

When he returned with his computer
and showed the pale images
a trapdoor opened inside me.
From the blank night a shadow materialized
into a cat – square jawed and calm,
it examined the camera, crouched, circled
and came to rest on the straw mat.

The man said 'panther' and I fell
into a lower sky, strange
safety, where night was made
manifest in our depleted family.

Then he advanced the frame.
The front door opened and I knew what I would see
would change me. I would no longer suffer
ideas about love, the living or the dead.
He said the shimmer in the air
was the camera's light reflecting from her hair
but I could see he was afraid.
I mumbled something like a prayer:
*protect, forgive, take me.*
In the next moment everything,
even the name I had given her,
escaped me as she appeared there."

# INCANTATION OF THE SPIRITS
## OF EARTH AND AIR
(*From Manfred*)

When the moon is on the wave,
   And the glow-worm in the grass,
And the meteor on the grave,
   And the wisp on the morass;
When the falling stars are shooting,
And the answer'd owls are hooting,
And the silent leaves are still
In the shadow of the hill,
Shall my soul be upon thine,
With a power and with a sign.

Though thy slumber may be deep,
Yet thy spirit shall not sleep;
There are shades which will not vanish,
There are thoughts thou canst not banish;
By a power to thee unknown,
Thou canst never be alone;
Thou art wrapt as with a shroud,
Thou art gather'd in a cloud;
And forever shalt thou dwell
In the spirit of this spell.

Though thou seest me not pass by,
Thou shalt feel me with thine eye
As a thing that, though unseen,
Must be near thee, and hath been;
And when in that secret dread
Thou hast turn'd around thy head,
Thou shalt marvel I am not
As thy shadow on the spot,
And the power which thou dost feel
Shall be what thou must conceal.

And a magic voice and verse
Hath baptized thee with a curse;
And a spirit of the air
Hath begirt thee with a snare;
In the wind there is a voice
Shall forbid thee to rejoice;
And to thee shall night deny
All the quiet of her sky;
And the day shall have a sun,
Which shall make thee wish it done.

From thy false tears I did distil
An essence which hath strength to kill;
From thy own heart I then did wring
The black blood in its blackest spring;
From thy own smile I snatch'd the snake,

For there it coil'd as in a brake;
From thy own lip I drew the charm
Which gave all these their chiefest harm;
In proving every poison known,
I found the strongest was thine own.

By thy cold breast and serpent smile,
By thy unfathom'd gulfs of guile,
By that most seeming virtuous eye,
By thy shut soul's hypocrisy;
By the perfection of thine art
Which pass'd for human thine own heart;
By thy delight in others' pain,
And by thy brotherhood of Cain,
I call upon thee! and compel
Thyself to be thy proper hell!

And on thy head I pour the vial
Which doth devote thee to this trial;
Nor to slumber, nor to die,
Shall be in thy destiny;
Though thy death shall still seem near
To thy wish, but as a fear;
Lo! the spell now works around thee,
And the clankless chain hath bound thee;
O'er thy heart and brain together
Hath the word been pass'd – now wither!

GEORGE GORDON, LORD BYRON (1788–1824)    139

*From* THE GHOSTS OF THE BUFFALOES

Last night at black midnight I woke with a cry,
The windows were shaking, there was thunder on high,
The floor was a-tremble, the door was a-jar,
White fires, crimson fires, shone from afar.
I rushed to the door yard. The city was gone.
My home was a hut without orchard or lawn.
It was mud-smear and logs near a whispering stream,
Nothing else built by man could I see in my dream ...
Then ...
Ghost-kings came headlong, row upon row,
Gods of the Indians, torches aglow.

They mounted the bear and the elk and the deer,
And eagles gigantic, aged and sere,
They rode long-horn cattle, they cried "A-la-la."
They lifted the knife, the bow, and the spear,
They lifted ghost-torches from dead fires below,
The midnight made grand with the cry "A-la-la."
The midnight made grand with a red-god charge,
A red-god show,
A red-god show,
"A-la-la, a-la-la, a-la-la, a-la-la."

With bodies like bronze, and terrible eyes
Came the rank and the file, with catamount cries,

Gibbering, yipping, with hollow-skull clacks,
Riding white bronchos with skeleton backs,
Scalp-hunters, beaded and spangled and bad,
Naked and lustful and foaming and mad,
Flashing primeval demoniac scorn,
Blood-thirst and pomp amid darkness reborn,
Power and glory that sleep in the grass
While the winds and the snows and the great rains pass.

They crossed the gray river, thousands abreast,
They rode in infinite lines to the west,
Tide upon tide of strange fury and foam,
Spirits and wraiths, the blue was their home,
The sky was their goal where the star-flags are furled,
And on past those far golden splendors they whirled.
They burned to dim meteors, lost in the deep.
And I turned in dazed wonder, thinking of sleep.

And the wind crept by
Alone, unkempt, unsatisfied,
The wind cried and cried –
Muttered of massacres long past,
Buffaloes in shambles vast . . .
. . . . . . . . .
The wind in the chimney

Seemed to say: –
"Dream, boy, dream,
If you anywise can.
To dream is the work
Of beast or man.
Life is the west-going dream-storm's breath,
Life is a dream, the sigh of the skies,
The breath of the stars, that nod on their pillows
With their golden hair mussed over their eyes."
The locust played on his musical wing,
Sang to his mate of love's delight.
I heard the whippoorwill's soft fret.
I heard a cricket carolling,
I heard a cricket carolling,
I heard a cricket say: "Good-night, good-night,
Good-night, good-night, ... good-night."

# THE DEAD KING EATS THE GODS

The sky is a dark bowl, the stars die and fall.
The celestial bows quiver,
the bones of the earthgods shake
and planets come to a halt
when they sight the king in all his power,
the god who feeds on his father and eats his mother.
The king is such a tower of wisdom
even his mother can't discern his name.
His glory is in the sky, his strength lies in the horizon,
like that of his father the sungod Atum who
        conceived him.
Atum conceived the king,
but the dead king has greater dominion.
His vital spirits surround him,
his qualities lie below his feet,
he is cloaked in gods and cobras coil on his forehead.
His guiding snakes decorate his brow
and peer into souls,
ready to spit fire against his enemies.
The king's head is on his torso.
He is the bull of the sky
who charges and vanquishes all.
He lives on the stuff of the gods,
he feeds on their limbs and entrails,
even when they have bloated their bodies with magic

at Nesisi, the island of fire.
The king is prepared
and his spirits are assembled
and he appears as the mighty one, Lord of Holy
    Ministers.
He is seated with his back to the earthgod Geb
and he passes judgment
with the One whose name is concealed
on this day when the Oldest Ones are slaughtered.
He dines on sacrificial meals,
binding the victims
in preparation for the feast.
The dead king eats men and lives on gods
and to carry messages he has couriers:
Kehau the Grasper of Horns lassoes them like oxen,
and Serpent with the Raised Head
oversees and drives the victims,
and Master of Bloody Sacrifice binds them.
The moongod Khons, Racer with Knives,
strangles them for the king
and draws out their entrails.
He is the courier the king sends to hold them bound.
Shezmu, the winepress god, slices them up
and cooks a supper for the king
in his evening hearth.
He is the one who feasts on their magic
and swallows their spirits.

The great ones are for breakfast,
the medium-size ones are for supper
and the tiny ones are for midnight treats.
Old men and women are burnt for incense.
The mighty stars in the northern sky
ignite fires under the cauldrons
with the thighs of their elders.
The sky-dwellers take care of him and sweep the hearth
with their women's legs.
He has traveled through the two firmaments
and walked both banks of the Nile.
He is omnipotent
and his power over the powerful is absolute.
He is a holy icon, the holiest of all icons of omnipotence
and he eats as raw meat
whomever he finds on his path.
He stands first on the horizon among the nobility,
a god older than the oldest.
Thousands are at his feet,
hundreds sacrifice to him.
Orion, father of the gods, assigned him his deed of
        power.
The dead king appears again in the heavens,
the crowned Lord of the Horizon.
He snapped their backbones, drained their marrow,
and tore out the hearts of the gods.
He ate the red crown worn by the King of Lower Egypt.

145

He swallowed the green crown of the goddess Wadjet,
guardian of Lower Egypt.
He feeds on the Wise Ones' lungs.
He is sated with their hearts and magic.
He won't lick the foul tasting substances of the red
        crown.
He flourishes and enjoys himself with the magic in
        his belly.
His dignities are inviolate.
He has swallowed the intelligence of every god.
The dead king lives forever.
His boundary is infinite.
He does as he pleases
since he inhabits the endless horizon.
Observe how their spirits fill his stomach.
Their souls belong to him.
He cooks the leftover gods into a bone soup.
Their souls belong to him
and their shadows as well.
In his pyramid among those who live on the earth
        of Egypt,
the dead king ascends and appears
forever and forever.

# DEVILS, GODS,
# ANGELS, DEATH

## *From* ZAHHAK'S BURNING TEHRAN

*"What is your name?" Zahhak asked the monster.*
*"My father named me Eblis!" the monster said.*

Zahhak and the Monster

Of old, in the Arabian deserts, dwelled
a king named Merdas, who in fear of God
shook as though shaken by a whipping wind.
This prince was large and generous and grand.
He had a son, a red-blooded youth, wide-
awake, whose name was Zahhak, and who'd ride
all day, galloping his horse with might
on rutted courses with his lusty drive.
One day, a monster, masked as a nomad, ran
to talk to Zahhak. With his simple soul,
the monster's words like siren songs began
to sway and twist his mind: "I have a deal
for you, some buried secrets and hush-hush
plans." "Tell me. Teach me!" Zahhak gushed.

They Dug a Big Pit

Before he'd tell him, Eblis made him vow
he wouldn't leak the scheme for anything.

The gypped youth pledged. Now Eblis spoke of
       the king:
"Why does that gray man reign? Let his son now
sit on that high seat." But love for father
froze Zahhak's mind; he begged for other schemes
than murder! "No, you *can't* renege," screamed
Eblis. At last, they framed how to fell the father.
The king had a big garden where he spent
hours praying in darkness. Eblis dug a pit
capped with hay. The servants did not light
lanterns up to give a clearer sight.
Inside the pit, Merdas's body lay.
Eblis filled the hole and walked away.


Eblis Turns Cook

Once Eblis saw that Zahhak took the crown,
he put on his second devilish act.
"The whole world's yours, if you make this next pact.
Want birds to swim, want fish to fly? You'll gain
your wish." Days later, Eblis changed to a young
tall man, sublime, smooth-tongued, and went to
       Zahhak
and spoke; "Sultan, I am a savvy cook,
the best cook in the region, and I long
to cook for you." "The royal kitchen's yours.

Give him our larder's keys." And the cook laid
his plan by making soup from a beast's blood,
but before he served the special course
he told the sultan: "I have a magic dish
and I can serve your Highness if you wish."


## Two Black Serpents

That night King Zahhak slept with his mind full
of this thought: "*What's* his mystic dish?" Next day,
the cook prepared a gorgeous partridge that lay
with a white pheasant on the tray, so well-
designed, with rose-water, saffron on top. He served
the feast with wine for the grand Sultan to partake.
Zahhak feasted and he said: "Well! Cook,
you may have whatever you desire."
"Sultan, you have my love. Might I kiss
your shoulders, rub them with my eyes and face?"
"May your fame grow, great cook. I grant your wish."
Eblis kissed the shoulders from the rear,
then dissolved. From the shoulders, two red snakes
thrust their heads out. His eyes bulged with fear.

## Hissing Fear

A fear had swallowed the room whole, compressed
the breath in their throats. And Eblis's melt-down to
the floor sank them in horror. Worse, those two
red-skinned snakes tore the flesh more to force
out their scaled trunks. Fear hatched in the king's drawn
face. The serpents turned their necks, and red
ghastly teeth protruded from the jaws.
When the mouths closed, those fanged teeth were still
    bared.
Golden sparkling scribbled lines were shining
on the arched and s-shaped trunks. The Sultan's men
blanched, and a white hissing fear glued Zahhak
to his grand seat, his nails clawing the lion
heads of the throne's arms. His coward knights
all hid. No one could speak, muted by fright.


## Feed Them Brains

From everyone, the king sought remedies
but finding none, he tried to cut them off.
Yet, just as branches shoot afresh from trees
these two black serpents sprang again out of
the royal shoulders. Learned physicians thronged
around. They weighed all kinds of witchcraft. But

now Eblis loomed among the hopeless throng.
He loudly, lordly, said to them "Tut-tut,"
and cleared his throat before berserk Zahhak,
masking himself this time as a physician.
"Fate has doomed you to this weird condition.
You don't cut the serpents off. You cook
them foods. What food? Nothing – I can't be clearer
– but *human brains*. They'll die this way. I swear."


The Shah of Iran

Eblis's design was to cleanse the world
of people; wash the world of brains that think.
At the same time a great disorder swirled
in the next country, in Iran, where the king,
Jamshid, made laws that warred with God's.
So God deprived Jamshid of his goodwill.
The Shah had always cleaved to God, was good,
but now he boasted, "Sunshine, sleep, tranquil-
lity all come through me. So who can claim
that anyone but *I* am king?" His allies
left him. He walked on the foul path of folly.
New kings sprang up to overthrow his reign.
Word from Arabia brought knights adventuring,
seeking to find the hellborn dragon king.

# FROM HELL, MISTER LUSK

Dante's *Inferno*, CANTO XII: The Violent

The seventh circle's more miles of animals lying down
than water, and this shade has all the pain
he wanted, in the color of dresses.

He's ankle-deep in a woman, the heat rearing
his half-horse body into her again and again.
And in this form, he's his own witness,

for the butcher's horse watched the last whore's
lace falling out of her, her growing less full
of her own sea, and she was the loveliest of all

so why not a lamp of her heart? And why not the
    breeze
around the window?

When first he heard the circle's hook
unshelving the ribs and lowering the stream,
he didn't know where his hands should go.

Azzolino moved back into the throat. Pyrrhus wept
through his mad search, where his legs were gone
inside the coarse flank and shaft

of his ass, his wide-awake hat dropping a stream
of small things: packet of cachous, mud,
a broken piece of comb, pieces of soap,

a metal spoon, some buttons, a fist
of clothes swallowed by the ford's
hungry milk. Hell was using arrows.

Hell was using arrows, and the caul
flung over his shoulders,
to stomach him.

## CANTO XIII: THE WOOD OF SUICIDES
(*From The Inferno*)

On every side, I heard wailing voices grieve,
Yet I could not see anyone there to wail,

And so I stopped, bewildered. I believe
My guide believed that in my belief the voices
I heard from somewhere in among the grove

Came somehow from people who were in hiding
    places –
And therefore the master said, "If you remove
A little branch from any one of these pieces

Of foliage around us, the thoughts you have
Will also be broken off." I reached my hand
A little in front of me and twisted off

One shoot of a mighty thornbush – and it moaned,
"Why do you break me?" Then after it had grown
Darker with blood, it began again and mourned,

"Why have you torn me? Have you no pity, then?
Once we were men, now we are stumps of wood:
Your hand should show some mercy, though we
    had been

The souls of serpents." As flames spurt at one side
Of a green log oozing sap at the other end,
Hissing with escaping air – so that branch flowed

With words and blood at once, at which my hand
Released the tip; and I stood like one in dread.
"Had he been able to credit or comprehend

Before, O wounded spirit," my sage replied,
"What he had seen only inside my verses,
His hand would never have performed this deed

Against you. But the fact belief refuses
Compelled me, though it grieves me, thus to prompt
    him.
But tell him who you are, so that his praises

May make amends by freshening your fame
When he returns again to the world above,
As he is granted." Answered the broken stem:

"Your words have so much sweetness they contrive
To draw me out of silence; I am enticed
To talk a little while – may it not prove

Burdensome to you. I am he who possessed
Both keys to Frederick's heart – and I turned either,
Unlocking and locking with so soft a twist

I kept his secrets from almost any other.
To this, my glorious office, I stayed so true
I lost both sleep and life. The harlot that never

Takes its whore's eyes from Caesar's retinue –
The common fatal Vice of courts – inflamed
All minds against me; and they, inflamed so,

So inflamed Augustus that the honors I claimed
In gladness were converted into pain.
My mind, in its disdainful temper, assumed

Dying would be a way to escape disdain,
Making me treat my juster self unjustly.
I swear by this tree's freshest roots, again:

I never betrayed my lord, who was so worthy
Of honor. If you return to the world above,
Either of you, please comfort my memory

Still prostrate from the blow that Envy gave."
The poet waited a moment, then said to me,
"Since he is silent, don't waste the time you have,

But speak, and ask him what you wish." And I:
"You question him, and ask what you discern
Would satisfy me; I cannot because of pity

That fills my heart." Therefore my guide began,
"For this man freely to do the thing you say,
Imprisoned spirit, tell him if you can

And if it pleases you, in just what way
The soul is bound in knots like these; give word
Also, if any soul could be set free

From members such as these." It puffed air hard,
And soon that exhalation became a voice:
"You shall be answered briefly then," it uttered.

"When the fierce soul has quit the fleshly case
It tore itself from, Minos sends it down
To the seventh depth. It falls to this wooded place –

No chosen spot, but where fortune flings it in –
And there it sprouts like a grain of spelt, to shoot
Up to a sapling, then a wild plant: and then

The Harpies, feeding on the foliage, create
Pain, and an outlet for the pain as well.
We too shall come like the rest, each one to get

His cast-off body, but not for us to dwell
Within again: for justice must forbid
Having what one has robbed oneself of – still,

Here we shall drag them; and through the mournful
      wood
Our bodies will be hung, with every one
Fixed on the thornbush of its wounding shade."

160   DANTE ALIGHIERI (1265–1321)
      TRANS. ROBERT PINSKY

# NIGHT OF HELL

I have swallowed a fabulous dose of poison. –
Thrice-blessed be the counsel given me! – My guts are
ablaze. The venom twists my limbs, deforms and
flattens me. I'm dying of thirst, I'm suffocating, I
cannot cry out. This is hell – eternal pain! See how the
fires flare up! I'm roasted to a turn. Atta boy, demon!

One time, I nearly caught a glimpse of conversion:
to goodness and happiness, salvation, etc. Can
I describe that vision now? hymns of praise are
forbidden here; the air won't carry them. In my vision
I saw a million charming creatures moving in time to
beautiful church-music, Power and Peace, noble
ambitions, and lord knows what.

Noble ambitions!

And still this is life! – So what if damnation *is*
forever and ever? A man who chooses to mutilate
himself deserves damnation, yes? I believe that I'm in
hell, so I'm in hell. So much for catechism. I'm the
slave of my own baptism. Parents, you made my life a
misery, and your lives too. Poor innocents! – Hellfire
can't harm heathens. – And still this is life! Later on,
the delights of damnation will be deeper. Quickly, a
crime, anything – so long as I can tumble into
nothingness, according to the law.

161

Shut up, shut up will you!...There's nothing but shame here, and reproach: Satan, who says fire is loathsome, that my anger is stupid. — Enough! ... Falsehoods they whisper to me, magic spells, cheap perfumes, childish music. — And to think that I possess truth, that I understand justice: I have a firm and certain mind, I'm ready for perfection... Arrogance. — My scalp is drying up. Have pity! Sweet Jesus, I'm afraid. I'm thirsty, so very, very thirsty! Ah! childhood, the grass, the rain, the lake upon the stones, *the moonlight at midnight when the bells were chiming*... the devil's in the belfry then. Mary! Blessed Virgin!... — My horrid stupidity.

162   ARTHUR RIMBAUD (1854–91)
TRANS. DONALD REVELL

## SATAN'S SPEECH TO THE FALLEN
## ANGELS
(*From Paradise Lost*)

"Thrones, Dominations, Princedoms, Virtues, Powers;
For in possession such, not only of right,
I call ye, and declare ye now; returned
Successful beyond hope, to lead ye forth
Triumphant out of this infernal pit
Abominable, accursed, the house of woe,
And dungeon of our tyrant: Now possess,
As Lords, a spacious world, to our native Heaven
Little inferior, by my adventure hard
With peril great achieved. Long were to tell
What I have done; what suffered; with what pain
Voyaged th' unreal, vast, unbounded deep
Of horrible confusion; over which
By Sin and Death a broad way now is paved,
To expedite your glorious march; but I
Toiled out my uncouth passage, forced to ride
The untractable abyss, plunged in the womb
Of unoriginal Night and Chaos wild;
That, jealous of their secrets, fiercely opposed
My journey strange, with clamorous uproar
Protesting Fate supreme; thence how I found
The new-created world, which fame in Heaven
Long had foretold, a fabric wonderful

Of absolute perfection! therein Man
Placed in a Paradise, by our exile
Made happy: Him by fraud I have seduced
From his Creator; and, the more to encrease
Your wonder, with an apple; he, thereat
Offended, worth your laughter, hath given up
Both his beloved Man, and all his world,
To Sin and Death a prey, and so to us,
Without our hazard, labour, or alarm;
To range in, and to dwell, and over Man
To rule, as over all he should have ruled.
True is, me also he hath judged, or rather
Me not, but the brute serpent in whose shape
Man I deceived: that which to me belongs,
Is enmity which he will put between
Me and mankind; I am to bruise his heel;
His seed, when is not set, shall bruise my head.
A world who would not purchase with a bruise,
Or much more grievous pain? – Ye have the account
Of my performance; what remains, ye Gods,
But up, and enter now into full bliss?"

So having said, a while he stood, expecting
Their universal shout, and high applause,
To fill his ear; when, contrary, he hears
On all sides, from innumerable tongues,
A dismal universal hiss, the sound

Of public scorn; he wondered, but not long
Had leisure, wondering at himself now more,
His visage drawn he felt to sharp and spare;
His arms clung to his ribs; his legs entwining
Each other, till supplanted down he fell
A monstrous serpent on his belly prone,
Reluctant, but in vain; a greater power
Now ruled him, punished in the shape he sinned,
According to his doom: he would have spoke,
But hiss for hiss returned with forkèd tongue
To forkèd tongue; for now were all transformed
Alike, to serpents all, as accessories
To his bold riot. Dreadful was the din
Of hissing through the hall, thick swarming now
With complicated monsters, head and tail,
Scorpion, and Asp, and Amphisbæna dire,
Cerastes horned, Hydrus, and Ellops drear,
And Dipsas; (not so thick swarmed once the soil
Bedropt with blood of Gorgon, or the isle
Ophiusa,) but still greatest he the midst,
Now Dragon grown, larger than whom the sun
Ingendered in the Pythian vale on slime,
Huge Python, and his power no less he seemed
Above the rest still to retain; they all
Him followed, issuing forth to the open field,
Where all yet left of that revolted rout,
Heaven-fallen, in station stood or just array;

Sublime with expectation when to see
In triumph issuing forth their glorious Chief;
They saw, but other sight instead! a crowd
Of ugly serpents; horror on them fell,
And horrid sympathy; for what they saw,
They felt themselves now changing; down their arms,
Down fell both spear and shield; down they as fast;
And the dire hiss renewed, and the dire form
Catched, by contagion; like in punishment,
As in their crime. Thus was the applause they meant,
Turned to exploding hiss, triumph to shame
Cast on themselves from their own mouths. There stood
A grove hard by, sprung up with this their change,
His will who reigns above, to aggravate
Their penance, laden with fair fruit, like that
Which grew in Paradise, the bait of Eve
Used by the Tempter: on that prospect strange
Their earnest eyes they fixed, imagining
For one forbidden tree a multitude
Now risen, to work them further woe or shame;
Yet, parched with scalding thirst and hunger fierce,
Though to delude them sent, could not abstain;
But on they rolled in heaps, and, up the trees
Climbing, sat thicker than the snaky locks
That curled Megæra: greedily they plucked
The fruitage fair to sight, like that which grew
Near that bituminous lake where Sodom flamed;

This more delusive, not the touch, but taste
Deceived; they, fondly thinking to allay
Their appetite with gust, instead of fruit
Chewed bitter ashes, which the offended taste
With spattering noise rejected: oft they assayed,
Hunger and thirst constraining; drugged as oft,
With hatefullest disrelish writhed their jaws,
With soot and cinders filled; so oft they fell
Into the same illusion, not as Man
Whom they triumphed once lapsed. Thus were they
    plagued
And worn with famine, long and ceaseless hiss,
Till their lost shape, permitted, they resumed;
Yearly enjoined, some say, to undergo,
This annual humbling certain numbered days,
To dash their pride, and joy, for Man seduced.

JOHN MILTON (1608–74)

# THE GARDENER

After the first astronauts reached heaven
the only god discovered in residence
retired to a little brick cottage
in the vicinity of Venus. He was not
unduly surprised. He had seen it coming
since Luther. Besides, what with the imminence
of nuclear war, his job was nearly over.
As soon as the fantastic had become
a commonplace, bus tours were organized
and once or twice a day the old fellow
would be trotted out from his reading of Dante
and asked to do a few tricks – lightning bolts,
water spouting from a rock, blood from a turnip.
A few of the remaining cherubim
would fly in figure eights and afterwards
sell apples from the famous orchard.
In the evening, the retired god would sometimes
receive a visit from his old friend the Devil.
They would smoke their pipes before the fire.
The Devil would stroke his whiskers and cover
his paws with his long furry tail. The mistake,
he was fond of saying, was to make them in
your image instead of mine. Perhaps, said
the ex-deity. He hated arguing. The mistake,
he had often thought, was to experiment

with animal life in the first place when
his particular talent was as a gardener.
How pleasant Eden had been in those early days
with its neat rows of cabbages and beets,
flowering quince, a hundred varieties of rose.
But of course he had needed insects and then
he made the birds, the red ones which he loved;
later came his experiments with smaller mammals –
squirrels and moles, a rabbit or two. When
the temptation had struck him to make something
really big, he had first conceived of it
as a kind of scarecrow to stand in the middle
of the garden and frighten off predators. What
voice had he listened to that convinced him
to give the creature his own face? No voice
but his own. It had amused him to make
a kind of living mirror, a little homunculus
that could learn a few of his lesser tricks.
And he had imagined sitting in the evening
with his friend the Devil watching the small
human creatures frolic in the grass. They would
be like children, good natured and always singing.
When had he realized his mistake? Perhaps
when he smiled down at the first and it
didn't smile back; when he reached down to help

it to its feet and it shrugged his hand aside.
Standing up, it hadn't walked on the paths marked
with white stones but on the flowers themselves.
It's lonely, God had said. So he made it a mate,
then watched them feed on each other's bodies,
bicker and fight and trample through his garden,
dissatisfied with everything and wanting to escape.
Naturally, he hadn't objected. Kicked out,
kicked out, who had spread such lies? Shaking
and banging the bars of the great gate, they had
begged him for the chance to make it on their own.

# MEPHISTOPHELES

Every Sunday they left a circus of dust behind them,
as they poured out on the turnpike in stately,
    overcrowded carriages,
and the showers found nobody at home,
and trampled through the bedroom windows.

It was a custom at these staid Sunday dinners
to serve courses of rain instead of roast-beef;
on the baroque sideboard, by the Sunday silver,
the wind cut corners like a boy on a new bicycle.

Upstairs, the curtain rods whirled, untouched;
the curtains rose like a salvo to the ceiling.
Outside the burghers kept losing themselves,
they showed up chewing straws by cow-ponds.

Later, when the long cortege of carriages
approached the city wall,
the horses shied
from the shadow of the Gothic gallows.

The devil in blood-red stockings with rose rosettes
danced along the sunset-watered road –
he was as red
as a boiling lobster.

One thought a snort of indignation
had ripped the lid of heaven
from the skyline's low vegetation;
the devil's ribbons fluttered and danced.

The carriages swam through his eyes like road-signs;
he scarcely lifted a finger in greeting.
He rolled on his heels, he rumbled with laughter,
he sidled off hugging Faust, his pupil.

TRANS. ROBERT LOWELL

# NEMESIS

Thro' the ghoul-guarded gateways of slumber,
    Past the wan-moon'd abysses of night,
I have liv'd o'er my lives without number,
    I have sounded all things with my sight;
And I struggle and shriek ere the daybreak, being
      driven to madness with fright.

I have whirl'd with the earth at the dawning,
    When the sky was a vaporous flame;
I have seen the dark universe yawning,
    Where the black planets roll without aim;
Where they roll in their horror unheeded, without
      knowledge or lustre or name.

I had drifted o'er seas without ending,
    Under sinister grey-clouded skies
That the many-fork'd lightning is rending,
    That resound with hysterical cries;
With the moans of invisible daemons that out of the
      green waters rise.

I have plung'd like a deer thro' the arches
    Of the hoary primordial grove,
Where the oaks feel the presence that marches
    And stalks on where no spirit dares rove;

And I flee from a thing that surrounds me, and leers
    thro' dead branches above.

I have stumbled by cave-ridden mountains
    That rise barren and bleak from the plain,
I have drunk of the fog-foetid fountains
    That ooze down to the marsh and the main;
And in hot cursed tarns I have seen things I care not
    to gaze on again.

I have scann'd the vast ivy-clad palace,
    I have trod its untenanted hall,
Where the moon writhing up from the valleys
    Shews the tapestried things on the wall;
Strange figures discordantly woven, which I cannot
    endure to recall.

I have peer'd from the casement in wonder
    At the mouldering meadows around,
At the many-roof'd village laid under
    The curse of a grave-girdled ground;
And from rows of white urn-carven marble I listen
    intently for sound.

I have haunted the tombs of the ages,
    I have flown on the pinions of fear
Where the smoke-belching Erebus rages,

Where the jokulls loom snow-clad and drear:
And in realms where the sun of the desert consumes
    what it never can cheer.

I was old when the Pharaohs first mounted
    The jewel-deck'd throne by the Nile;
I was old in those epochs uncounted
    When I, and I only, was vile;
And Man, yet untainted and happy, dwelt in bliss on
    the far Arctic isle.

Oh, great was the sin of my spirit,
    And great is the reach of its doom;
Not the pity of Heaven can cheer it,
    Nor can respite be found in the tomb:
Down the infinite aeons come beating the wings of
    unmerciful gloom.

*Thro' the ghoul-guarded gateways of slumber,*
    *Past the wan-moon'd abysses of night,*
*I have liv'd o'er my lives without number,*
    *I have sounded all things with my sight;*
*And I struggle and shriek ere the daybreak, being driven*
    *to madness with fright.*

What sphinx of cement and aluminum bashed open
   their skulls and ate up their brains and
   imagination?
Moloch! Solitude! Filth! Ugliness! Ashcans and
   unobtainable dollars! Children screaming under
   the stairways! Boys sobbing in armies! Old men
   weeping in the parks!
Moloch! Moloch! Nightmare of Moloch! Moloch the
   loveless! Mental Moloch! Moloch the heavy
   judger of men!
Moloch the incomprehensible prison! Moloch the
   crossbone soulless jailhouse and Congress of
   sorrows! Moloch whose buildings are judgment!
   Moloch the vast stone of war! Moloch the
   stunned governments!
Moloch whose mind is pure machinery! Moloch whose
   blood is running money! Moloch whose fingers
   are ten armies! Moloch whose breast is a cannibal
   dynamo! Moloch whose ear is a smoking tomb!
Moloch whose eyes are a thousand blind windows!
   Moloch whose skyscrapers stand in the long
   streets like endless Jehovahs! Moloch whose
   factories dream and croak in the fog! Moloch
   whose smokestacks and antennae crown the
   cities!

Moloch whose love is endless oil and stone! Moloch
    whose soul is electricity and banks! Moloch
    whose poverty is the specter of genius! Moloch
    whose fate is a cloud of sexless hydrogen! Moloch
    whose name is the Mind!
Moloch in whom I sit lonely! Moloch in whom
    I dream Angels! Crazy in Moloch! Cocksucker in
    Moloch! Lacklove and manless in Moloch!
Moloch who entered my soul early! Moloch in whom
    I am a consciousness without a body! Moloch
    who frightened me out of my natural ecstasy!
    Moloch whom I abandon! Wake up in Moloch!
    Light streaming out of the sky!
Moloch! Moloch! Robot apartments! invisible suburbs!
    skeleton treasuries! blind capitals! demonic
    industries! spectral nations! invincible
    madhouses! granite cocks! monstrous bombs!
They broke their backs lifting Moloch to Heaven!
    Pavements, trees, radios, tons! lifting the city to
    Heaven which exists and is everywhere about us!
Visions! omens! hallucinations! miracles! ecstasies!
    gone down the American river!
Dreams! adorations! illuminations! religions! the
    whole boatload of sensitive bullshit!

Breakthroughs! over the river! flips and crucifixions!
      gone down the flood! Highs! Epiphanies!
      Despairs! Ten years' animal screams and suicides!
      Minds! New loves! Mad generation! down on the
      rocks of Time!
Real holy laughter in the river! They saw it all! the
      wild eyes! the holy yells! They bade farewell!
      They jumped off the roof! to solitude! waving!
      carrying flowers! Down to the river! into the
      street!

# THE WHALE
*From The Middle English Physiologus*

The whale's the biggest fish upon the sea,
You see it float near, and think it must be

An island planted on the ocean floor.
When this enormous creature hungers for

A meal, its mouth gapes wide, its throat gives birth
To what must be the sweetest scent on earth,

So other fish are drawn to him in bliss
And linger in his mouth; not knowing this

A trap, they are sucked in, and when he snaps
His great jaws shut, small fish become his snacks.

In this way tiny fish become deceived,
Though bigger fish of course will not be seized.

This fish dwells healthily on the sea ground
Until a hurricane stirs things around

And the deep water's so disturbed the whale
Must rise and surface and wait out the gale

Which tosses ships about with turbid strife.
The sailors who dread death and live for life

See the whale and think it is an isle
Where they can shelter from the storm a while.

They moor upon it and with stone and steel
They kindle tinder and cook up a meal.

Warmed by the fire, joyful, they eat and drink
But the fire burns the whale, who starts to sink,

And once he dives down to the ocean's ground
The sailors all are drowned without a wound.

*The Significance*

The Devil's powerful and schooled in wile
Like witches filled with sorcery and guile.

He makes men full of thirst and ravenous
For every kind of sin, desire and lust.

He draws the small ones with flowered breath
But once drawn in they find disgrace and death

The small ones have weak faith; only the great
In spirit and in flesh evade this fate.

Hear the Devil and you will not end well.
The hope you anchor there drags you to hell.

180    ANON. (*c.*1250)
       TRANS. TONY BARNSTONE

# THE WHALE

Greatest of fish inhabiting the ocean waste
  Is the whale. Sprawling on the tide the beast
Looks like a mountain or an island on the sea,
  Which mariners imagine him to be.
When he is famished and desires to feed on fish,
  He opens his great mouth and with a swish
Expels a breath tasting of flowery perfume
  So he can lure the little fish to come,
Only the tiny ones (for those more fully grown
  He cannot catch or even swallow down),
And these swim in his jaws before he gulps them all,
  Unlike the fish who swallowed Jonah whole.

When summer flame and violent storms infect the air,
  Muddying and troubling the ocean floor,
The monster shoots up to the surf and lies serene
  Where as a promontory he is seen.
Then sailors, tossed and driven, sight the peaceful form
  And rope their ship to it against the storm.
They leap ashore and start a fire with some wood,
  Warming themselves and heating up their food,
But when the monster feels the blaze he swiftly dives,
  Sinking the ship, and robs them of their lives.

Now the Devil is huge in body like the mammoth whale
    And to some men he imparts his magic skill.
Throughout the world he petrifies the minds of men
    And thirsts for all he can corrupt; and when
He finds the weak in faith he uses candied words –
    Though by the strong in faith he is unheard.
He who confides his hope in him is coarsely heaved
    Down into Hell and bitterly deceived.

182  BISHOP THEOBALDUS (11TH CENTURY)
    TRANS. WILLIS BARNSTONE

*From* THE DEVIL'S WALK

1.

From his brimstone bed, at break of day,
   A-walking the Devil is gone,
To look at his little, snug farm of the World,
   And see how his stock went on.

2.

Over the hill and over the dale,
   And he went over the plain;
And backward and forward he swished his tail,
   As a gentleman swishes a cane.

3.

How, then, was the Devil dressed?
   Oh! he was in his Sunday's best;
His coat was red, and his breeches were blue,
And there was a hole where his tail came through.

4.

A lady drove by in her pride,
In whose face an expression he spied,
   For which he could have kissed her;
Such a flourishing, fine, clever creature was she,
With an eye as wicked as wicked can be,
"I should take her for my Aunt," thought he,
   "If my dam had had a sister."

5.

    He met a lord of high degree, –
    No matter what was his name, –
Whose face with his own when he came to compare
    The expression, the look, and the air,
    And the character too, as it seemed to a hair, –
    Such a twin-likeness there was in the pair,
    That it made the Devil start and stare;
For he thought there was surely a looking-glass there,
    But he could not see the frame.

6.

He saw a Lawyer killing a viper
    On a dunghill beside his stable:
"Ho!" quoth he, "thou put'st me in mind
    Of the story of Cain and Abel."

7.

An Apothecary on a white horse
    Rode by, on his vocation;
And the Devil thought of his old friend
    Death in the Revelation.

8.

He passed a cottage with a double coach-house,
    A cottage of gentility;
And he owned with a grin
That his favorite sin
    Is pride that apes humility.

9.

He saw a pig rapidly
  Down a river float:
The pig swam well, but every stroke
  Was cutting his own throat; —

10.

And Satan gave thereat his tail
  A twirl of admiration;
For he thought of his daughter War,
  And her suckling babe Taxation.

11.

Well enough, in sooth, he liked that truth,
  And nothing the worse for the jest;
But this was only a first thought,
  And in this he did not rest:
Another came presently into his head;
And here it proved, as has often been said,
  That second thoughts are best.

12.

For as Piggy plied, with wind and tide,
  His way with such celerity,
And at every stroke the water dyed
With his own red blood, the Devil cried,
"Behold a swinish nation's pride
  In cotton-spun prosperity!"

13.

He walked into London leisurely;
    The streets were dirty and dim;
But there he saw Brothers the Prophet,
    And Brothers the Prophet saw him.

14.

He entered a thriving bookseller's shop:
    Quoth he, "We are both of one college;
For I myself sate like a Cormorant once
    Upon the Tree of Knowledge."

15.

As he passed through Cold-Bath Fields, he looked
    At a solitary cell;
And he was well pleased, for it gave him a hint
    For improving the prisons of Hell.

# LUCIFER IN STARLIGHT

On a starr'd night Prince Lucifer uprose.
  Tired of his dark dominion swung the fiend
  Above the rolling ball in cloud part screen'd,
Where sinners hugg'd their spectre of repose.
Poor prey to his hot fit of pride were those.
  And now upon his western wing he lean'd,
  Now his huge bulk o'er Afric's sands careen'd,
  Now the black planet shadow'd Arctic snows.
Soaring through wider zones that prick'd his scars
  With memory of the old revolt from Awe,
He reach'd a middle height, and at the stars,
Which are the brain of heaven, he look'd, and sank.
Around the ancient track march'd, rank on rank,
  The army of unalterable law.

GEORGE MEREDITH (1828–1909)

*From FAUST*

FAUST. And what have you to give, poor devil!
 Has any human spirit and its aspirations
 ever been understood by such as you?
 Of course you've food that cannot satisfy,
 gold that, when held, will liquefy
 quicksilverlike as it turns red,
 games at which none can ever win,
 a girl who, even in my arms, will with her eyes
 pledge her affections to another,
 the godlike satisfaction of great honor
 that like a meteor is gone at once.
 Show me the fruit that, still unplucked, will rot
 and trees that leaf each day anew!
MEPHISTOPHELES. These commissions don't
  dismay me,
 I can oblige you with such marvels.
 But, friend, there also comes a time when we prefer
 to savor something good in peace and quiet.
FAUST. If on a bed of sloth I ever lie contented,
 may I be done for then and there!
 If ever you, with lies and flattery,
 can lull me into self-complacency
 or dupe me with a life of pleasure,
 may that day be the last for me!
 This is my wager!

MEPHISTOPHELES. Here's my hand!

FAUST.                                    And mine again!
  If I should ever say to any moment:
  Tarry, remain! – you are so fair!
  then you may lay your fetters on me,
  then I will gladly be destroyed!
  Then they can toll the passing bell,
  your obligations then be ended –
  the clock may stop, its hand may fall,
  and time at last for me be over!

MEPHISTOPHELES. Consider well your words – we'll
    not forget them.

FAUST. Nor should you! What I've said
  is not presumptuous blasphemy.
  If I stagnate, I am a slave –
  why should I care if yours or someone else's?

MEPHISTOPHELES. This very day at the doctoral
    banquet,
  I'll do my duty as your servant.
  One other matter! – as insurance
  I must request a line or two in writing.

FAUST. So you want something written, too, you
    pedant?
  Have you not ever known a man whose word was
    good?

Is it not enough that my spoken word
grants perpetual title to my days?
Do not the tides of life race on unceasing –
how could a promise obligate me!
But still our hearts have their illusions,
and who would care to live without them?
Happy the man whose heart is loyal to his pledges –
he'll not be grieved by any sacrifice they ask.
And yet, a parchment document that bears a seal –
that is a spectre that all people shun.
The word begins to die before it's left the pen,
and wax and goatskin take control.
What do you, evil spirit, want from me –
marble or brass, foolscap or parchment?
Am I to write with chisel, stylus, pen?
You are at liberty to choose.

MEPHISTOPHELES. How can you work yourself up so
    quickly
to this heat of rhetorical exaggeration?
Any small scrap of paper is all right.
A tiny drop of blood will do to sign your name.

FAUST. If this is all that you require,
we may as well go through with the tomfoolery.

MEPHISTOPHELES. Blood is a very special juice.

# HADES' PITCH

*If I could just touch your ankle,* he whispers, *there
on the inside, above the bone* — leans closer,
breath of lime and peppers — *I know I could
make love to you.* She considers
this, secretly thrilled, though she wasn't quite
sure what he meant. He was good
with words, words that went straight to the liver.
Was she falling for him out of sheer boredom —
cooped up in this anything-but-humble dive, stone
gargoyles leering and brocade drapes licked with fire?
Her ankle burns where he described it. She sighs
just as her mother aboveground stumbles, is caught
by the fetlock — bereft in an instant —
while the Great Man drives home his desire.

RITA DOVE (1952–)                                          191

# DEVIL'S TATTOO

Who fired first
into my household
the black death
of the leather bat-wing?
Who breathed low-voiced,
"My Lord and my God"?

Who dropped the stitch
that weakened the chain
that split the hair
that opened the loophole?
A curse on the joiner
that plied the board
that contained the knot-hole.

His mouth has the smell
of musk, his body
of autumn flowers.
A sweet gas
dissolves from him
through the room's air.

His eyes burn a sunset
in a horizontal smokescreen,
ice-water through
the veins of my dream.

The tip of his tongue
down the brush of the telephone
lassoes my nape.
A pillar of cloud
pulls me by day,
a pillar of fire by night.

Till my morning sickness
dawns on me for the first time:
why half-dead groping
for his love-bites on my neck,

I come across these scraped on
paper scraps that were my sheets.

NUALA NÍ DHOMHNAILL (1952–)
TRANS. MEDBH McGUCKIAN AND
EILÉAN NÍ CHUILLEANÁIN

# IN THE PINES

Vertical spindles of shadow, the black
Firs & violet pines surround
This open meadow broken
Only by a pond
Illuminated like an old Bible
With flakes of gold leaf; & beside
The pond, a hunter's decrepit shack
I've claimed, its split planks
Chinked with plaster & old rags. Just
Today, I've spent
The morning poking out a bird's nest
Lodged in the crooked brick chimney
Pointing up
Through the roof like a single
Broken finger . . . Here, the only
Accusing voices are those
Of the branches snapping & smoking
In the stove, of the gray squirrels chasing
The one albino out of their trees
To, I imagine,
Some ghetto of oak or maple
Reserved for him; & look, his tail
Is as erect as a white feather
Pen, a plume dipped into its tiny, snowy
Inkwell, the spine of the tail quivering

As the fronds of hair
Are blown by a rising breeze. Here,
I can do as I wish; that is, nothing.
I was told the words
I could use most tactfully
With relatives & friends included, *"recovery"*
& *"recuperation,"* or even, *"a simple rest,"*
The doctor said while handing my last
Check to his indifferent nurse.
Fuck them all, I thought,
I'm never coming back. Besides, they have
No way of knowing
I have a "friend" now, though
She is beyond – & I mean this quite
Literally – any description they might
Understand. I first heard her singing
One evening at dusk
As I began to boil the water
For my coffee. I was sure it was a song
I knew though couldn't place, & the singer's
Voice was more lovely than any
I could remember…When I stepped out
Into the clearing, walking a few yards
Along the muddy lip of the pond,
I could see her sitting

High in the branches of a tall, nearby pine;
Slowly, her wings – blond wings the breadth
Of a man's body – began to work
So beautifully & rhythmically to the song
She sang
                that she rose
Out of the pines, circling above the cabin
& the pond, circling lower, lower
Until I could see she had a woman's face,
The whole shining head of a woman . . .
Long wheat-colored hair
Floating back over her arced wings;
& her face just wasn't any woman's face,
It was a face even more delicate & lovely
Than her song. Her body was the body
Of a condor: just as powerful, graceful, sleek . . .
& though I knew her name
From childhood books, from my father's
Leather-bound *Bullfinch*, I knew
That name was wrong, absolutely wrong, so
Very absurd & wrong. She
Was so much more like an angel, if more
Beautiful than any I could have dreamed;
There was no question: *like an angel.*
For three days,
She came each evening to the pond
& sang for me; then, on the fourth night,

She disappeared . . . Thank God that now,
As dusk has just begun to fall, I can
See that she's returned to sit
In the stiff, umber limbs of the pine
At the clearing's edge, a pine I watched
Shiver & sway, but never fall, as lightning
Touched it, in the summer's first
Electric storm. In these days
That she's been gone, her song's grown
So much sadder; yet

                    I know it now by heart,
Its endless double stairways, its empty
Circular courts. This evening,
I'll call her down to the fallen oak by
The pond, coaxing her to rest in its low branches
While I stroke her hair, running my hands
From the narrow slope
Of her shoulders down along her delicate
Spine, over the long white-&-gold feathers
Falling limply from the small of
Her back. I'll lift those feathers, letting
Them spread across my chest like the damp fan
Of an emperor's courtesan, the tips
Of the long feathers
Cutting my neck like fine razors
As I unbuckle my pants & pull myself
Into her, her talons gripping

The long scarred branches of the oak
& with each thrust of my body –
Her body arching back into mine . . .
At last, I know
Our motion together is more than angel
& man, bird & man, world & man . . .
Her wings begin unfolding beneath me
As I lean forward, my mouth closing on
The fine gold down swirling
At the nape of her neck –
We rise slowly out of the oak, the long
Strokes of her wings forcing our bodies
To lock tightly together; I will not
Let myself look back
Until I know we're far above the needles of
The pines, far above the high range marking
The horizon. Yet, when I do look,
I can see the smoke of my
Dinner fire still rising from the bent
Brick finger; the cabin roof, with its random
Squares of tar & plastic, looks so lovely,
Like a child's patchwork quilt thrown casually
Over the quiet, suddenly still crib . . . Then,
She begins to sing again, very
Softly at first;
As we climb, I can see
                    the rocks below

Are topped by tiny caps of snow, the air
Tasting of minerals, of rain...
& I know soon now
She'll tire of my weight, tire of
Lifting any man this near the empty heavens;
& I know my lungs in this clarity of air
Will last no longer than
Her song. Though I hardly care, though
I foresaw it all, still,
I know as well as she knows – in stories
Of this kind – when what comes
Has come finally to its end, which of us
Must fall...

## DEMONS

The moon through total darkness hurrying
Illuminates the snow in flight;
Clouds are whirling, clouds are scurrying,
Dark is the sky, and dark the night.
Across the open plain I'm driven;
The little bell goes *Ding-ding-ding* . . .
By holy dread my soul is riven,
Such emptiness is gathering.

"Coachman, drive them faster, faster! . . ."
"Can't, sir; they're too tired, you see;
I'm blinded by the blizzard, master;
The roads are drifting heavily;
Can't see the horses — lost the track, sir;
We're done for — we'll be frozen — whey! . . .
Some demon's got us — that's a fact, sir!
A demon's leading us astray.

Look, there he is! He's teasing, blowing,
Spitting at me . . . Lord! this one's mean —
He's scared the horses — they'll be going
Headlong into some damned ravine;
He's right in front — Lord, isn't he frightening!
Dressed like a milestone (bloody queer);
There he goes, off again, like lightning!
God save us, master — that was near."

The moon through total darkness hurrying
Illuminates the snow in flight;
Clouds are whirling, clouds are scurrying,
Dark is the sky, and dark the night.
We lurch in circles, strength declining;
Suddenly silent is the bell;
The team has halted ... "What's that shining?" ...
"Tree-stump or wolf, sir – who can tell?"

The storm is howling, the storm is crying,
Drives itself harder, in despair;
The horses snort; away he's flying,
Only his eyes in the grey murk flare;
The horses strain upon their traces;
The little bell goes *Ding-ding-ding*...
I see, amidst the endless spaces,
A host of spirits, gathering.

Numberless and formless devils
In the blizzard's moonlit haze
Twirling in their murky revels,
As leaves swirl in November days ...
So many! So many! And being carried
Whither? Why do they plaintively sing?
Is there a witch who's getting married?
Some goblin are they burying?

The moon through total darkness hurrying
Illuminates the snow in flight;
Clouds are whirling, clouds are scurrying,
Dark is the sky, and dark the night.
Swarm upon swarm of demons, streaking
On through this limbo without end,
And with their plaintive howls and shrieking
They pounce upon my heart, and rend.

## DEUS EX MACHINA

Because it rained inside the house
and became a house of tears
there were plastic buckets
and pans and pots and porcelain teacups
scattered everywhere filling with water.
Thimbles were set out to catch
the smallest drops.
I heard the sound of rain
or the sound of crying
and everything
– even the apples and figs –
tasted like salt.
One day I asked,
as I stood knee deep in water
in the middle of my bedroom,
"Is this a tragedy, this house?"
Sunday morning,
at the moment when my bed
began to float like a raft,
the great red tractor
drove up to my door with its headlights on
illuminating the Christian day.
As though it were bringing fire,
smoke poured out of its exhaust stack
and the sound of the potent diesel motor was thunder.

God drove the giant machine
that came to rib and plant
and harvest and rake
the wet, graveyard
earth of my house.

*From* THE OLDEST LEGEND OF
ANCESTORS
(*Oral epic of the De Ang people*)

III.
Just as the darkness starts to fade
   the earth starts to flood.
The fifty-one pairs of brothers and sisters cry out
   and wake up the wise Padaran.
He yawns and stretches and breaks the earth up
   and lets water run down its crevices.
He brings the wind
   and asks the other sisters and brothers of the tea
     plant to help.
They pile up nine thousand nine hundred and ninety
     feet high of tea leaves
   and break the gate of heaven open.
The leaves ride the clear wind and chase the flood.
Wherever there are tea leaves the flood recedes.
The earth is exposed.
The hills of Deang become fertile and fragrant
   because they are created with piles of bodies of their
     ancestors.
Every hill brings forth the golden fruit of their
     ancestors.

The tea leaves have chased the flood far away.
The land stretches long and wide.
The brothers and sisters are happy.
Padaran appears above the cloud on the sky.
"Heaven wants to set up east, west, north and south
    so the earth will have four directions.
And there will be peaks, valleys, mountains and rivers
And there will be warmth, heat, cold, and ice.
Padaran decrees at times when he feels too hot
    there will be a place for taking a bath."

The leaf brothers and sisters stop.
And turn to go back to heaven.
They are tired.
And their steps become slower and slower.
The strong ones walk ahead.
The weak ones lie on the path.
The leaves become thicker and thicker.
The earth becomes thicker and thicker.
When they return to the gate of heaven,
    it has been closed . . .

The earth gains nine lakes and eighteen oceans.
Those are the places Padaran bathes.
Thus the earth retains one thousand rivers and ten
    thousand lakes
    because the tears of the brothers and sisters
    continue.

Far from the sea there rises a high peak.
It is the highest place on earth.

The flood recedes completely.
The sky is glass-blue.
The brothers and sisters look down at the earth.
The earth becomes a strange place
    full of crazy demons.
Four of the devils look the same:
    three heads and six hands, four eyes and eight feet.
The new born earth is suffering at the feet of the
        demons and devils.

To save the earth from the evil spirits,
    the brothers and sisters go down again to fight with
        them.
The red devil spurts out fire.
The white devil spits out thick fog.
The black demon spews plague.
The yellow demon splashes poison.
The fire burns and the fog hurts eyes.
The plague kills and the poison maims.
The brothers in the front fall to the ground.
The sisters in the back run back to heaven.

The sisters worry about their brothers.
They bite their fingers and grind their teeth.

Their eyes run blood and tears.
They pray their brothers return to safety
     after getting rid of the demons.
They beg the moon to give them the silver bow,
     and the sun to give them the golden arrow.
To bring the clear wind from the gate of heaven
And the stars with their sharp ray.

The rainbow cloud floats under the sisters.
The sun, the moon, and the stars lend their helping
          hands.
The golden arrow shoots down the burning fire.
The clear wind blows the fog away.
The sharp ray melts the dark poison.
The silver lightning kills the plague.
The four demons are defeated.
Their bodies are cut up into sixteen parts.
The sky returns to the brightness of crystal amber.

The sisters call out to their brothers.
Their voices crisp as the mountain stream.
They caressed their brothers.
Their feelings hot like fire.
The brothers are filled with warmth.
They open their eyes.
They stretch out their arms.
They straighten their backs.

They are alive.
The brothers and sisters are happy.
The sisters dance and celebrate.
The brothers sing the song of resurrection.
The singers and the dancers forget
    the four horrible devils.

The devils rise again
    and turn the sky and the earth into chaos once more.
The brothers and sisters are again in peril.
They fight bravely with their bare hands.
They can't forgive the once-defeated demons.
The hard-learned lesson can't be forgotten.

The brothers fight on ground.
The sisters help in the sky.
They fight for three thousand years
    and only bring down one demon.
They fight for six thousand years
    and defeat two of them.
They fight for nine thousand years
    and bring down the death on them all.
The earth cannot return to chaos again.
The happy time has to be restored.
Brothers dig holes in earth.
Sisters bury the devils in the ground.

ANON. (ANCIENT)                                        209
TRANS. CLAIRE WANG-LEE (WANG KE-NAN)
AND MICHELLE MITCHELL-FOUST

## SONNET 100

In night when colors all to black are cast,
Distinction lost, or gone down with the light;
The eye a watch to inward senses placed,
Not seeing, yet still having powers of sight,

Gives vain alarums to the inward sense,
Where fear stirred up with witty tyranny,
Confounds all powers, and thorough self-offense,
Doth forge and raise impossibility:

Such as in thick depriving darknesses,
Proper reflections of the error be,
And images of self-confusednesses,
Which hurt imaginations only see;

And from this nothing seen, tells news of devils,
Which but expressions be of inward evils.

# THE SECOND COMING

Turning and turning in the widening gyre
The falcon cannot hear the falconer;
Things fall apart; the centre cannot hold;
Mere anarchy is loosed upon the world,
The blood-dimmed tide is loosed, and everywhere
The ceremony of innocence is drowned;
The best lack all conviction, while the worst
Are full of passionate intensity.

Surely some revelation is at hand;
Surely the Second Coming is at hand.
The Second Coming! Hardly are those words out
When a vast image out of Spiritus Mundi
Troubles my sight: a waste of desert sand;
A shape with lion body and the head of a man,
A gaze blank and pitiless as the sun,
Is moving its slow thighs, while all about it
Wind shadows of the indignant desert birds.

The darkness drops again but now I know
That twenty centuries of stony sleep
Were vexed to nightmare by a rocking cradle,
And what rough beast, its hour come round at last,
Slouches towards Bethlehem to be born?

WILLIAM BUTLER YEATS (1865–1939)          211

## BEAST FROM THE SEA
(*From* The Book of Revelation)

Then I saw a beast coming up from the sea,
With ten horns and seven heads and on his horns
Ten diadems, and on his heads were the names
Of blasphemy. The beast I saw was like a leopard,
His feet like a bear and his mouth like the mouth
Of a lion. And the dragon gave him his power
And his throne and fierce power of dominion.

One of his heads seemed to be stricken to death
But the wound causing his death was healed
And the whole world marveled after the beast.
They worshiped the dragon since he had given
Dominion to the beast, and they worshiped the beast,
Saying, "Who is like the beast and can battle him?"

He was given a mouth to speak great things
And blasphemies. And he was given dominion
To act for forty-two months. Then he opened
His mouth to utter blasphemies against God,
Blaspheming his name and his tenting place,
And those who have set their tent in the sky.

He was given powers to battle the saints
And to overcome them, and was given powers

Over every tribe and people and tongue and nation.
All who dwell on the earth will worship him,
Each one whose name has not been written since
The foundation of the world in the book of life
Of the slaughtered lamb. Who has an ear, hear
    Yirmiyahu:
He who leads into captivity goes into captivity.
He who kills with the sword will be killed by the sword.
Such is the endurance and faith of the saints.

ANON. (LATE 1ST–EARLY 2ND CENTURY)          213
TRANS. WILLIS BARNSTONE

# THE WORLD

By day she woos me, soft, exceeding fair:
    But all night as the moon so changeth she;
    Loathsome and foul with hideous leprosy
And subtle serpents gliding in her hair.
By day she woos me to the outer air,
    Ripe fruits, sweet flowers, and full satiety:
    But through the night, a beast she grins at me,
A very monster void of love and prayer.
By day she stands a lie: by night she stands
    In all the naked horror of the truth
With pushing horns and clawed and clutching hands.
Is this a friend indeed; that I should sell
    My soul to her, give her my life and youth,
Till my feet, cloven too, take hold on hell?

# INCUBUS

Eyes glowing like an angel's
I'll come back to your bed
and reach for you from the shadows:
you won't hear a thing.

On your dark skin my kisses
will be colder than moonlight:
caresses of a snake crawling
round an open grave.

When the morning whitens
you find no one beside you:
the place cold all day.

Others by fondness prevail
over your life, your youth:
I leave it to fear.

CHARLES BAUDELAIRE (1821–67)                215
TRANS. RICHARD HOWARD

# ENKIDU'S DREAM OF THE UNDERWORLD
(*From The Epic of Gilgamesh*)

Enkidu drifted through layers of hazy
half-sleep, his fists clenched, his stomach queasy.
At dawn he turned to Gilgamesh,
relating his dream. "Last night the cloudless
sky was broken by a low moan.
The earth howled its frenzied response, and I stood
    alone
between them. A figure rose before me,
a towering, darkened body,
formed from a lion's head and paws,
and an eagle's talons reaching to claw
my loose hair. I beat him, struggled with him,
but his body overpowered mine.
As he grasped me, I called to you,
Gilgamesh, but you were too
frightened, watching this man trample me.
But then he transformed my body,
and my arms grew feathered and as graceful as a bird's.
He clutched one of my wings and led me down to
    Irkalla's
palace, the House of Shades.
Those who enter that place never return.
They walk down a road but never return.
They sit huddled in darkness, hidden from all light,
eating clay and mud, swallowing dust and dirt.

Like birds they cover their limbs with feathered clothes,
and layers of dust settle on the door's thick bolt.
Scattered heaps of crowns clutter the floor:
dead kings who ruled the earth before
hover in the doorways, transformed,
waiting only to serve steaks brimming with red juice
and cool pure water to Enlil and Anu.
I entered the House of Ash
where I saw the high priest and the wailer,
the purification priest and the dervish,
and the priest of the Great Gods.
Etana and Sumuquan were there, and
so was Ereshkigal, Queen of the Underworld.
Belit-Seri, the Underworld's scribe,
knelt before her, reading aloud from her writing tablet
where everyone's fate is inscribed.
Ereshkigal lifted her head, looked me in the eyes
and asked, 'Who has brought this man here?' "

"Your dream is terrifying," Gilgamesh replied.
Curled on his bed Enkidu lay
growing ever more ill day after day.
On the twelfth day, he struggled to lift his head,
calling to Gilgamesh, "Friend, the gods are angry.
I am cursed, not even able
to die gracefully in battle."
Then Gilgamesh heard the death rattle
and he moaned for his friend like a dove.

ANON. (*c.* 2000 BCE)                                    217
VERSION BY TONY BARNSTONE
AND EMMA VARESIO

# THE LAND OF THE DEAD
(*From The Odyssey*)

"Then I addressed the blurred and breathless dead,
vowing to slaughter my best heifer for them
before she calved, at home in Ithaca,
and burn the choice bits on the altar fire;
as for Teiresias, I swore to sacrifice
a black lamb, handsomest of all our flock.
Thus to assuage the nations of the dead
I pledged these rites, then slashed the lamb and ewe,
letting their black blood stream into the well pit.
Now the souls gathered, stirring out of Erebus,
brides and young men, and men grown old in pain,
and tender girls whose hearts were new to grief;
many were there, too, torn by brazen lanceheads,
battle-slain, bearing still their bloody gear.
From every side they came and sought the pit
with rustling cries; and I grew sick with fear.
But presently I gave command to my officers
to flay those sheep the bronze cut down, and make
burnt offerings of flesh to the gods below –
to sovereign Death, to pale Persephone.
Meanwhile I crouched with my drawn sword to keep
the surging phantoms from the bloody pit
till I should know the presence of Teiresias....

Soon from the dark that prince of Thebes came forward
bearing a golden staff; and he addressed me:

" 'Son of Laertes and the gods of old,
Odysseus, master of landways and seaways,
why leave the blazing sun, O man of woe,
to see the cold dead and the joyless region?
Stand clear, put up your sword;
let me but taste of blood, I shall speak true.'

"At this I stepped aside, and in the scabbard
let my long sword ring home to the pommel silver,
as he bent down to the somber blood."

HOMER (9TH–8TH CENTURY BCE)                    219
TRANS. ROBERT FITZGERALD

# ADDRESS
(*From* Suite for Emily)

Hello Death Angel, old familiar, old nemesis.
   In the deepest hours, I have recognized
your floating shape. I've seen your breath
   seduce the torn curtain
masking the empty window, have crouched with you
   in the doorway, curled in the alley
hooded in your essence & shadow, have
   been left blue, heart-stopped
for yours, for yours. Death,
   you are the bead in the raptor's eye,
Death you dwell in the funneling depths
   of the heavens beyond each
star's keening shrill, Death you are the potion
   that fills the vial, the night
the monuments have swallowed. You live
   in the maimed child wrapped in a wreckage
of headlines. Death you center
   in the fanged oval
of the prison dog's howl. Death you dwell within
   the necropolis we wake to in nightmare's
hot electric wind. You glint
   the edge of the boy's razor,
patient in the blasted stairwell. Everywhere
   you walk deep lawns, TVs pollinating air

with animals wired up to dance
    for their food, with executions
& quiz shows. You're in the column
    of subway wind roaring before each
train's arrival. I've seen you drape thoughtlessly
    a woman's hair over her face
as the shot carried her forward into stop-time
    & beyond anything she's laid
her money down for. Death your sliver works
    swiftly through the bloodstream.
Hello Death Angel, Plague is your sister.
    I've seen her handiwork, heard
the tortured breath, watched her loosen the hands
    of the dazzling boys from each other.
For love, love. I've seen the AIDS hotels
    & sick ones begging homeless
in the tunnels, the whispered conspiracies.
    Shameless emissaries with your powders
& wands, your lunar carnivorous flowers.
    Tricks, legerdemain. I've seen you draw
veined wings over the faces of sleepers,
    the abandoned, the black feather that sweeps
so tenderly. I've seen the stain you scribe
    on the pavement, the glossy canopy of leaves

you weave. I've seen waste & ruin, know
 your kingdom for delirium, the furious thumbprints
you've scored on the flesh of those you choose.

 I've seen you slow-dance in a velvet mask, dip
& swirl across dissolving parquet.

 I've seen you swing open the iron gate –
a garden spired in valerian, skullcap, blue vervain.

 Seen you stir in the neat half-moons, fingernails
left absently in a glazed dish.

 Felons, I've cursed you in your greed, have spat
& wept then acquiesced in your wake. Without rue
 or pity, you have marked the lintels & blackened
the water. Your guises multiply, bewildering
 as the firmament's careless jewelry.
Death I have welcomed you to the rooms
 where Plague has lain when the struggle is passed
& lit the candles and blessed the ash.

 Death you have taken my friends & dwell
with my friends. You are the human wage.

 Death I am tired of you.

## NO. 712 (BECAUSE I COULD NOT STOP FOR DEATH)

Because I could not stop for Death –
He kindly stopped for me –
The Carriage held but just Ourselves –
And Immortality.

We slowly drove – He knew no haste
And I had put away
My labor and my leisure too,
For His Civility –

We passed the School, where Children strove
At Recess – in the Ring –
We passed the Fields of Gazing Grain –
We passed the Setting Sun –

Or rather – He passed Us –
The Dews drew quivering and Chill –
For only Gossamer, my Gown –
My Tippet – only Tulle –

We paused before a House that seemed
A Swelling of the Ground –
The Roof was scarcely visible –
The Cornice – in the Ground –

Since then – 'tis Centuries – and yet
Feels shorter than the Day
I first surmised the Horses' Heads
Were toward Eternity –

# FLUTE PLAYING THE DEATH OF THISBE
(*From A Midsummer Night's Dream*)

Asleep, my love?
What, dead, my dove?
O Pyramus, arise!
Speak, speak. Quite dumb?
Dead, dead? A tomb
Must cover thy sweet eyes.
These lily lips,
This cherry nose,
These yellow cowslip cheeks,
Are gone, are gone:
Lovers, make moan:
His eyes were green as leeks.
O Sisters Three,
Come, come to me,
With hands as pale as milk;
Lay them in gore,
Since you have shore
With shears his thread of silk.
Tongue, not a word:
Come, trusty sword;
Come, blade, my breast imbrue:
[*Stabs herself*]
And, farewell, friends;
Thus Thisby ends:
Adieu, adieu, adieu.

WILLIAM SHAKESPEARE (1564–1616)

# DEATH, TO THE DEAD FOR EVERMORE

Death, to the dead for evermore
A King, a God, the last, the best of friends –
Whene'er this mortal journey ends
Death, like a host, comes smiling to the door;
Smiling, he greets us, on that tranquil shore
Where neither piping bird nor peeping dawn
Disturbs the eternal sleep,
But in the stillness far withdrawn
Our dreamless rest for evermore we keep.

For as from open windows forth we peep
Upon the night-time star beset
And with dews for ever wet;
So from this garish life the spirit peers;
And lo! as a sleeping city death outspread,
Where breathe the sleepers evenly; and lo!
After the loud wars, triumphs, trumpets, tears
And clamour of man's passion, Death appears,
And we must rise and go.

Soon are eyes tired with sunshine; soon the ears
Weary of utterance, seeing all is said;
Soon, racked by hopes and fears,
The all-pondering, all-contriving head,
Weary with all things, wearies of the years;
And our sad spirits turn toward the dead;
And the tired child, the body, longs for bed.

## SKELETON

You hold onto the mantle
of my hips, knit them to yours.
Underneath, the jutted bones
of the pelvis, the iliac crest, sculpted
like a seashell. Your hands
grasp the knobs – the skeleton,
fibrous and calcified, soon enough
stripped clean without the canvas
of skin, red strip of muscle,
the jellied yellow tissue.
These bones, at last naked
like winter branches. The hips,
ribs, and skull – the inside finally
out. The eye sockets emptied –
no longer a lookout.
Like the last page of a book,
holding the air of already having seen.
Emptied of recognition – emptied
of capillaries mapping the eyelids red.
Emptied of the fistfuls of flesh
in your hands. Emptied of this moment –
the intermission of tension and delight,
the silver quiver of the almost.

SUZANNE ROBERTS (1970–)                    227

# INSTRUCTIONS FOR A JOURNEY

There are no provisions, but your guide
may teach you hymns during the long flight.
Sing lauds and benedictions on all nights
to soothe the guards of houses, one inside

the other. Take your journal, and a pen,
staplers, and dictionaries when you travel.
The landscape may appear unusual:
gray birds sail low; birches are frozen bones.

Prepare to see men seventy miles high,
their shoulders parasangs apart, with many heads
and tongues. All measurements are odd. Their eyes
flash lightning. Then the terror, as your body

assumes new forms, abandoning old molds.
First Heaven: Go through Customs and Security.
You'll see blunt hills the color of chalcedony.
Igneous water flows in riverbeds.

Chapels have stained-glass windows cut in moonstone,
marked "war" and "peace." Angels who pacify
the world praise God; they are condemned to die
if they sing louder than men, or out of tune.

In Sixth Heaven, angels of wrath and silence
greet you. Cherubs and seraphim dance;
gazelles with dappled faces flank the throne;
light strikes the trembling heart. You are alone.

You'll see a god of fire trailing stars,
then climb to see the chariot throne, and still
survive unharmed. Through blinding flame, through
     water,
you'll enter seven heavens and fall, whole.

# THE ANGEL OPENED

Nails through the gold shimmering
tips of the red wingspan across
the tree, stretched still,
the eyes black with color.
I stroke its body, its shudders
and twists, then split the chest,
examine the graceful ribs and veins
then pluck out the heart,
hold it, perfect, just covering my eye.
To walk these echoing chambers:
what a finely detailed joy,
what endless mirrors
and the nightmare finally opened
into a dark but open room.
I kiss the small throb
and toss it in the dirt while
the feathery eyes stare at me
and I run away singing
through all the chambers of the world,
hands glowing with tenderness,
wings, wings.

# QUESTIONS ABOUT ANGELS

Of all the questions you might want to ask
about angels, the only one you ever hear
is how many can dance on the head of a pin.

No curiosity about how they pass the eternal time
besides circling the Throne chanting in Latin
or delivering a crust of bread to a hermit on earth
or guiding a boy and girl across a rickety wooden
       bridge.

Do they fly through God's body and come out singing?
Do they swing like children from the hinges
of the spirit world saying their names backwards and
       forwards?
Do they sit alone in little gardens changing colors?

What about their sleeping habits, the fabric of their
       robes,
their diet of unfiltered divine light?
What goes on inside their luminous heads? Is there
       a wall
these tall presences can look over and see hell?

If an angel fell off a cloud, would he leave a hole
in a river and would the hole float along endlessly
filled with the silent letters of every angelic word?

If an angel delivered the mail, would he arrive
in a blinding rush of wings or would he just assume
the appearance of the regular mailman and
whistle up the driveway reading the postcards?

No, the medieval theologians control the court.
The only question you ever hear is about
the little dance floor on the head of a pin
where halos are meant to converge and drift invisibly.

It is designed to make us think in millions,
billions, to make us run out of numbers and collapse
into infinity, but perhaps the answer is simply one:
one female angel dancing alone in her stocking feet,
a small jazz combo working in the background.

She sways like a branch in the wind, her beautiful
eyes closed, and the tall thin bassist leans over
to glance at his watch because she has been dancing
forever, and now it is very late, even for musicians.

# ISIS UNVEILED

LONDON, 1977

The Indian café and the occult bookstore
that had been forgotten by time,
which is immaterial, are gone,

and so are the endless rainy afternoons
when I sat reading – or trying to read –
the mystical tracts of the Golden Dawn

that so inspired Yeats and Maud Gonne,
while a cranky one-armed waiter
played chess by himself in the corner.

I sipped steaming cups of spiced tea
and despaired over the leaden prose
of a system I couldn't crack,

Isis hidden behind too many veils
and Reality fogged like the city itself.
Even the windows seemed Rosicrucian.

Outside, the side streets were crooked
fingers, indexes pointing nowhere,
tucked in sleeves, dead-ends.

The Indian café and the occult bookstore
and the dreamy skeptic I was
are inside me still, and so is the night

I carried my books through a labyrinth
of mysterious buildings, obscure signs,
and ended up on the edge of a vast park

where the sky suddenly brightened
overhead, a west wind lifted
the wet leaves from the wet ground

and trees shimmered in the distance
like the airy shades of women
dancing in black slips.

## TO KITTY, WHO LOVED THE SEA
## AND SOMERSET MAUGHAM

The angel who smells of my childhood
My mother, piano and oboe
Whose face the icon reflects
Auburn hair like a Modigliani
Eyes the color of rain
Light caught by surprise
Whose presence the absence reveals
Whose laughter is burning snow
Whose warm breath I breathed
This morning as I woke
The scent of gardenias that whisper
*I never left you*

# HALO

1.

In the desert, a halo around the sun, a vast, prismed disk
with within it another smaller though still huge second circle,
of a slightly darker hue, the furnacing glare precisely in its center.

Suspended above us, so much a different scale from anything here,
it seems not merely light refracted, but some more solid substance;
it *weighs*, and instead of dissipating like an ordinary rainbow,

it stays intact, looms, forebodes, becomes a possible threat,
the outcome of an error, an incipient retaliation, who knows what for?
Perhaps something so dire it shouldn't be thought of.

2.

In a book in the Fifties, the then famous Jesuit scientist
Teilhard de Chardin posited a theory this puts me in mind of:
a bubble around the earth, a "noosphere" he called it,

consisting of all the yearnings, prayers, pleas, entreaties,
of humans for something beyond – he meant god, of course,
Christ – towards which he believed the universe was evolving.

Ingenious: an extra-material layer, numinous, literalized –
he'd even made drawings – very seductive for people like me,
who had no god, no Christ, but thought they might like to.

   3.
I still do, sometimes, wish I could believe. More often,
I'd like the whole holiness business gone once and for all,
the reflexive referencing to what I know isn't there,

the craving for retribution for the unjust at the end of the chain.
It's resistant as rock, though, like trying to get shed of the myth
of Adam and Eve, who you know can't be real, to put in their stead

the pair of sooty, stinking, starving Cro-Magnons
    who are.
Those bed-time stories, those nightmares, feel
    hammered
like nails into my mind, sometimes it seems they
    might *be* mind.


   4.

Now this, a puncture in the heavens, a rent, a tear,
aglow at the edges but dull within, matte, unreflecting,
a great open thing, like an eye; some sensory Cyclops

perceiving all but attentive to nothing (*blind*, I think,
    *numb*),
that makes us believe there are matters not to be
    thought of,
gaps within and between us, fissures, abysses,

that only leaps of forgiveness might span, might heal.
An angelless halo, the clear gore of light pouring
    through
without meaning or reason: *blind*, I think, *numb*.

*From* PSALM 18

I love you, O Lord, my strength.
The Lord is my rock, my fortress, and my deliverer, my
      God, my rock in whom I take refuge, my shield,
      and the horn of my salvation, my stronghold.
I call upon the Lord, who is worthy to be praised, so
      I shall be saved from my enemies.
The cords of death encompassed me; the torrents of
      perdition assailed me;
the cords of Sheol entangled me; the snares of death
      confronted me.
In my distress I called upon the Lord; to my God
      I cried for help. From his temple he heard my
      voice, and my cry to him reached his ears.
Then the earth reeled and rocked; the foundations also
      of the mountains trembled and quaked, because
      he was angry.
Smoke went up from his nostrils, and devouring fire
      from his mouth; glowing coals flamed forth from
      him.
He bowed the heavens, and came down; thick darkness
      was under his feet.
He rode on a cherub, and flew; he came swiftly upon
      the wings of the wind.
He made darkness his covering around him, his
      canopy thick clouds dark with water.

Out of the brightness before him there broke through
　　his clouds hailstones and coals of fire.
The Lord also thundered in the heavens, and the Most
　　High uttered his voice.
And he sent out his arrows, and scattered them; he
　　flashed forth lightnings, and routed them.
Then the channels of the sea were seen, and the
　　foundations of the world were laid bare at your
　　rebuke, O Lord, at the blast of the breath of your
　　nostrils.
He reached down from on high, he took me; he drew
　　me out of mighty waters.
He delivered me from my strong enemy, and from
　　those who hated me; for they were too mighty
　　for me.
They confronted me in the day of my calamity; but the
　　Lord was my support.
He brought me out into a broad place; he delivered
　　me, because he delighted in me.

# GOD OF THE GAS CHAMBERS,
# WHERE ARE YOU HIDING?

Yahweh, what do you have in mind while Jews
drop naked in chambers or the graves
they dig in Poland or Ukraine? Who saves
the souls of women, babies, when the ooz-
ing gas screams in their lungs? Or blasts of lead
lay them out under the non-mountain of
the night? When doctors die, when tailors spread
their arms, imploring you, where is that love
for us who are of mud like you? But since
you are like us, we are the lice of dawn,
floating in oily lakes while you, the prince
of darkness, drink our blood. Please go. I am
a cousin of the slaughtered, not the clone
of swine. Die off to keep alive the lamb.

## THE REFINERY

*"... our language, forged in the dark by centuries of violent pressure, underground, out of the stuff of dead life."*

Thirsty and languorous after their long black sleep
The old gods crooned and shuffled and shook their
    heads.
Dry, dry. By railroad they set out
Across the desert of stars to drink the world
Our mouths had soaked
In the strange sentences we made
While they were asleep: a pollen-tinted
Slurry of passion and lapsed
Intention, whose imagined
Taste made the savage deities hiss and snort.

In the lightless carriages, a smell of snake
And coarse fur, glands of lymphless breath
And ichor, the avid stenches of
Immortal bodies.

Their long train clicked and sighed
Through the gulfs of night between the planets
And came down through the evening fog
Of redwood canyons. From the train
At sunset, fiery warehouse windows

Along a wharf. Then dusk, a gash of neon:
*Bar.* Black pinewoods, a junction crossing, glimpses
Of sluggish surf among the rocks, a moan
Of dreamy forgotten divinity calling and fading
Against the windows of a town. Inside
The train, a flash
Of dragonfly wings, an antlered brow.

Black night again, and then
After the bridge, a palace on the water:

The great Refinery – impossible city of lights,
A million bulbs tracing its turreted
Boulevards and mazes. The castle of a person
Pronounced alive, the Corporation: a fictional
Lord real in law.

Barbicans and torches
Along the siding where the engine slows
At the central tanks, a ward
Of steel palisades, valved and chandeliered.

The muttering gods
Greedily penetrate those bright pavilions –
Libation of Benzene, Naphthalene, Asphalt,

Gasoline, Tar: syllables
Fractioned and cracked from unarticulated

Crude, the smeared keep of life that fed
On itself in pitchy darkness when the gods
Were new – inedible, volatile
And sublimated afresh to sting
Our tongues who use it, refined from oil of stone.

The gods batten on the vats, and drink up
Lovecries and memorized Chaucer, lines from movies
And songs hoarded in mortmain: exiles' charms,
The basal or desperate distillates of breath
Steeped, brewed and spent
As though we were their aphids, or their bees,
That monstered up sweetness for them while they
        dozed.

# MONSTERS I'VE MET

I met a ghost, but he didn't want my head,
He only wanted to know the way to Denver.
I met a devil, but he didn't want my soul,
He only wanted to borrow my bike awhile.
I met a vampire, but he didn't want my blood,
He only wanted two nickles for a dime.
I keep meeting all the right people –
At all the wrong times.

SHEL SILVERSTEIN (1930–99)

# ACKNOWLEDGMENTS

Thanks are due to the following copyright holders for permission to reprint:

ADDONIZIO, KIM: "Night of the Living, Night of the Dead" from *Tell Me.* Copyright © 2000 by Kim Addonizio. Reprinted with the permission of The Permissions Company, Inc. on behalf of BOA Editions, Ltd, www.boaeditions.org BAER, WILLIAM: "All Hallows Eve" © William Baer. Reprinted with the kind permission of the poet. BARNSTONE, TONY: "Enkidu's Dream of the Underworld" (from *The Epic of Gilgamesh*, translation by Tony Barnstone and Emma Varesio); "The Dead King Eats the Gods" (translation of ancient Egyptian text by Willis Barnstone and Tony Barnstone); "The Whale" (anonymous, from *The Middle English Physiologus*, translated by Tony Barnstone); "Los compadritos muertos" ("Dead Hoodlums") (from *El otro, el mismo* by Jorge Luis Borges, translated by Tony Barnstone). Reprinted with permission from Tony Barnstone. BARNSTONE, WILLIS: "God of the Gas Chambers, Where Are You Hiding?" by Willis Barnstone; "The Whale" (poem by Bishop Theobaldus / translation by Willis Barnstone); 'The Dead King Eats the Gods' (translation of ancient Egyptian text by Willis Barnstone and Tony Barnstone), reprinted with permission from Willis

253

255